Scripture Alive in Your Classroom with Drama

Sandra Watters

WESTBOW®
PRESS
A DIVISION OF THOMAS NELSON
& ZONDERVAN

Scriptures marked NKJ are taken from the New King James version, NKJ. Copyright © 1979, 1980,1982 by Thomas Nelson, Inc. Used by permission. All rights reserved.

Scriptures marked by NLT are taken from the Holy Bible, New Living Translation, NLT. Copyright © 1996, 2004, 2007 Tyndale House Foundation. Used by permission by Tyndale House Publishers, Inc., Carol Stream, Illinois 60188. All rights reserved.

Scriptures marked NIV are taken from the The Holy Bible, New International Version ®, NIV®. Copyright © 1973, 1978, 1984, 2011 by Biblica, Inc.™ Used by permission. All rights reserved worldwide.

Scriptures marked by ESV are taken from The ESV® Bible (The Holy Bible, English Standard Version®), Copyright © 2001 by Crossway, a publishing ministry of Good News Publishers. Used by permission. All rights reserved.

Scriptures marked by TLB are taken from The Living Bible, Copyright © 1971. Used by permission Tyndale House Publishers, Inc. Wheaton, Illinois 60189. All rights reserved.

Scriptures marked by NET are taken from The NET Bible® Copyright © 2005 by Biblical Studies Press, L.L.C., www.NETBIBLE.COM. Scripture quoted by permission. All Rights Reserved.

WestBow Press books may be ordered through booksellers or by contacting:

WestBow Press
A Division of Thomas Nelson & Zondervan
1663 Liberty Drive
Bloomington, IN 47403
www.westbowpress.com
1 (866) 928-1240

ISBN: 978-1-4908-6111-1 (sc)
ISBN: 978-1-4908-6112-8 (e)

Library of Congress Control Number: 2014922056

Printed in the United States of America.

WestBow Press rev. date: 1/5/2015

Contents

NEW TESTAMENT

About The Author

Sandra Bryan Watters was born in Princeton, West Virginia. She gave her life to Christ at a very early age. She married her high school sweetheart and they had their first child two years later. It was at that time that she began serving the Lord through church ministries. Currently, she has three grown children, eight grandchildren, and 2 great grandchildren. Sandra and her husband live in Fort Mill, South Carolina and are active members at GraceLife Church of Pineville in Pineville, North Carolina. She has worshiped and served in various ministries there for more than 50 years.

Sandra loves working with children and taught in her church for many years while her own children were young. She dropped teaching for a while to serve in other ministries until one day about eleven years ago there was a class of fifth graders without a teacher. She felt God nudging her to take that class and she has been teaching fifth graders since then. Although the church bought packaged curriculum for teaching, she felt the students needed more focus on the scriptures. Thus, the idea of *Scripture Alive in Your Classroom With Drama* was born.

A Big Thank You!!!!

I would like to thank the following:

God - for giving us His Word, the command to share It, and that it is recorded in such a way that it can be shared using drama.

My husband, James - He encourages me to teach the 5th grade. He helps with the financing of this project as well as creating the props. It is a joy working with him in this ministry.

My Daughter, Amy - She generously contributed her ideas and computer skills.

My sons, Jimmy and Bryan - They use their carpentry skills to create props when I need them.

Nancy Herring for proof reading the book. She did a wonderful job.

My Church, GraceLife Church of Pineville in Pineville, North Carolina – They allow me the freedom to teach. They continue to encourage me and provide storage space for my ever increasing props inventory.

Pastor Rodney Cripps - He has encouraged me in the writing of this book. His vast knowledge of the Bible has been an inspiration to me and I go to him often as a sounding board.

The parents of my students - They allow me to teach their fifth graders each week and often encourage me with their kind words.

Patricia Wooten, the wife of my pastor many years ago - She taught me in Sunday School in my early adult years. When she heard about my teaching the scriptures with drama, she encouraged me to publish this book.

A Word From the Author

When I began teaching the fifth graders several years ago, I was using the purchased curriculum that the church bought. While it was good material and the students were enjoying the games and activities, they were not learning the scriptures. When I started using the Bible to create scripts for the students to become the characters in the stories, they really began to understand the scriptures. Seeing the scriptures come to life for the students has been a highlight of my life.

I believe that the year my students spend in my classroom will have a lasting impact on them. Becoming the characters of the Bible every week will help them remember the scriptures and apply it to their own lives. I have received many thank you notes from my students thanking me for being their best teacher ever. For this, I give God all the praise.

I, of course, used these dramas for a fifth grade class, but they can be used for older students as well. This book is in no way complete with every story of the Bible. I have included the dramas that my class has enjoyed through the years. You don't have to look far into the Old Testament to find a story with lots of action and suspense.

My prayer is that *Scripture Alive in Your Classroom With Drama* will give you the tools you need to inspire your students.

Let's get started...

I didn't start out with a room full of props. I began with a few pieces of cloth and headbands for headgear. Hopefully, when the people of your church hear about your endeavor, they will assist you with props. One lady in our church has crocheted beards for the characters. Another lady designed and made several robes for my costumes. Over time, I have purchased many inexpensive items from a store with 'Dollar' in its name and I store them to use over and over again.

There are certainly many ways to create props for these dramas. Any of these scripts could be used for large event productions, such as churchwide events, and big elaborate props could be created. I, however, wanted to use drama on a weekly basis in my 5th grade class where time is limited. The tips in this book are designed to give you ideas for making props out of items you might already have available in your classrooms or can purchase relatively inexpensively and can be used over and over again.

Don't worry about having the perfect props, your kids have great imaginations. Frequently, I allow the students that arrive early to create the props needed for the set. Sometimes the students beat me to the classroom because they are so excited to help.

Tips From the Author

- If time allows, repeat the drama a second time. By the second run, students know where the scene changes are and what props to have ready at just the right time. My students always enjoy the second run through better than the first.

- Many of the props and scenes can be made using upholstery material. I visited an upholstery shop and they were happy to give me remnants from their supply.

- Many of the props and scenes can be created using your classroom furniture. A table turned upside down will make a nice boat or even a lion's den.

- Many of the stories take place in or near a river. Once you create a river that works well in your classroom, you will use it over and over again. I use a blue sheet for mine.

- Many of the stories take place at multiple locations. I find it useful to designate an area in the room for each location and mark them with simple signs on the wall.

- Many of the stories take place over several days or weeks or even years. I often dim the lights for a few seconds to show the passage of time.

- If you find yourself without a certain prop, just ask the students to improvise or use "pretend props." They are very creative and don't mind playing pretend.

OLD TESTAMENT

Adam and Eve Sin

Genesis 3: 1-23 (NET)

You will need:

Actors

    Narrator

    Adam

    Eve

    God

    Serpent

Props

    Tree

    Apple

Tips:

- Use a large plant or have a student hold a branch for the Tree of Life.
- Use fig leaves cut from paper for the actors to hold over their clothes.

Set the scene:

Adam and Eve are living in this beautiful garden that God gave them to occupy. They had everything. They had each other and all the food they needed. They did not have to work for any of it.

Discussion ideas:

- Adam and Eve failed to follow God's rules and commands. What happened? What happens when we fail to follow God's commands today?
- Satan tempted Eve and succeeded in getting her to sin, and he has been working to get people to sin ever since. How could Eve have resisted temptation? What can we do to resist temptation today?
- Adam blamed his sin on Eve, and Eve blamed hers on the serpent. How easy is it for us to excuse our sin by blaming someone else or our circumstances? We need to be responsible for our own actions and ask God to give us the strength and courage when we are tempted.

Narrator	Now the serpent was more shrewd than any of the wild animals that the Lord God had made. And he said to the woman...
Serpent	Is it really true that God said, 'You must not eat of any tree of the orchard?'
Eve	We may eat of the fruit from the trees of the orchard; but concerning the fruit of the tree that is in the middle of the orchard, God said, 'You must not eat from it, and you must not touch it, or else you will die.'
Serpent	Surely you will not die. For God knows that when you eat from it your eyes will open and you will be like divine beings who know good and evil.
Narrator	When the woman saw that the tree produced fruit that was good for food, was attractive to the eye, and was desirable for making one wise, she took some of its fruit and ate it. She also gave some of it to her husband who was with her, and he ate it. Then the eyes of both of them opened, and they knew they were naked; so they sewed fig leaves together and made coverings for themselves. Then the man and his wife heard the sound of the Lord God moving about in the orchard at the breezy time of the day, and they hid from the Lord God among the trees of the orchard. But the Lord God called to the man and said to him.
God	Where are you?
Adam	I heard you moving about in the orchard, and I was afraid because I was naked; and so I hid.
God	Who told you that you were naked? Did you eat from the tree that I commanded you not to eat from?
Adam	The woman whom you gave me, she gave me some fruit from the tree and I ate it.
God	[to Eve] What is this you have done?
Eve	The serpent tricked me, and I ate.

God   [turning to the serpent] Because you have done this, cursed are you above all the wild beasts and all the living creatures of the field! On your belly you will crawl and dust you will eat all the days of your life. And I will put hostility between you and the woman and between your offspring and her offspring, her offspring will attack your head, and you will attack her offspring's heel.

[turning to Eve] I will greatly increase your labor pains, with pain you will give birth to children. You will want to control your husband, but he will dominate you.

[turning to Adam] Because you obeyed your wife and ate from the tree about which I commanded you, 'You must not eat from it,' cursed is the ground thanks to you; in painful toil you will eat of it all the days of your life. It will produce thorns and thistles for you, but you will eat the grain of the field. By the sweat of your brow you will eat food until you return to the ground, for out of it you were taken; for you are dust, and to dust you will return.

Narrator   The man named his wife Eve, because she was the mother of all the living. The Lord God made garments from skin for Adam and his wife, and clothed them.

God   Now that the man has become like one of us, knowing good and evil, he must not be allowed to stretch out his hand, and take also from the tree of life and eat, and live forever.

Narrator   So the Lord God expelled him from the orchard in Eden to cultivate the ground from which he had been taken.

Cain and Abel

Genesis 4: 1-16 (NET)

You will need:

Actors   Props

     Narrator   Abel (non-speaking)

     Lord   Fruit (Cain's sacrifice)

     Eve   Animal (Abel's sacrifice)

     Cain

Tips:

- Use pictures of fruit or an animal if either is not available.
- Designate an area for the field.

Set the scene:

Adam and Eve had two sons, Cain and Abel.

Discussion ideas:

- Have you ever been jealous of someone? Jealousy arises when we compare ourselves or what we have to others. Why was Cain jealous of Abel?
- Why do you think the Lord respected Abel's offering and not Cain's? Perhaps it was Cain's attitude or the fact that it was not his best sacrifice. God was pleased with Abel's offering. We are asked to give of our time and resources to serve God. Is God happy with our sacrifice and our attitude in which we serve?

Narrator   Now the man had marital relations with his wife Eve, and she became pregnant
              and gave birth to Cain.

Eve   I have created a man just as the Lord did!

Narrator   Then she gave birth to his brother Abel. Abel took care of the flocks, while Cain
              cultivated the ground. At the designated time Cain brought some of the fruit of
              the ground for an offering to the Lord. But Abel brought some of the firstborn
              of his flock-even the fattest of them. And the Lord was pleased with Abel and
              his offering, but with Cain and his offering he was not pleased. So Cain became
              very angry, and his expression was downcast.

Lord   Why are you angry, and why is your expression downcast? Is it not true that if
              you do what is right, you will be fine? But if you do not do what is right, sin is
              crouching at the door. It is desires to dominate you, but you must subdue it.

Narrator   Now Cain talked to his brother Abel.

Cain   Let's go out to the field.

Narrator   While they were in the field, Cain attacked his brother Abel and killed him.

Lord   Where is your brother Abel?

Cain   I don't know. Am I my brother's guardian?

Lord   What have you done? The voice of your brother's blood is crying out to me
              from the ground! So now, you are banished from the ground, which has opened
              its mouth to receive your brother's blood from your hand. When you try
              to cultivate the ground it will no longer yield its best for you. You will be a
              homeless wander on the earth.

Cain   My punishment is too great to endure! Look! You are driving me off the land
              today, and I must hide from your presence. I will be a homeless wanderer on
              the earth; whoever finds me will kill me.

Lord   Alright then, if anyone kills Cain, Cain will be avenged seven times as much.

Narrator Then the Lord put a special mark on Cain so that no one who found him would strike him down. So Cain went out from the presence of the Lord and lived in the land of Nod, east of Eden.

The Flood
Genesis 6:9 – 8:12 (NLT)

You will need:

Actors   Props
    Narrator   Ark/Boat
    God   Dove
    Noah (non-speaking)   Many stuffed animals
    Shem (non-speaking)   Altar
    Ham (non-speaking)   Rainbow
    Japheth (non-speaking)
    Wife of Shem (non-speaking)
    Wife of Ham (non-speaking)
    Wife of Japheth (non-speaking)

Tips:

- Remind students to act as the narrator tells the story.
- Turn a table upside down for the ark.
- Ask students to bring their stuffed animals.
- Assign a student to "operate" the dove.
- Altar can be created by stacking boxes or stones.
- Have a student hold up a picture of a rainbow at the appropriate time.

Set the scene:

People had become corrupt and violent and God was angry with everyone.

Discussion ideas:

- Does God hate sin? So much so, that he destroyed the earth because the people had filled it with so much sin.

- Noah was asked to do something that involved a lot of work and made him unpopular. Have you ever been asked to do something that would cause you to become unpopular? How did you handle it? Noah obeyed God, even when it was hard, and God blessed him. God is faithful to those who obey Him.
- What was the first thing Noah did after leaving the ark? He built an altar to offer a sacrifice to God. Offering a sacrifice was a way of worshiping God. When God brings us through difficult situations, we need to take time to worship and give praise to Him.

Narrator   This is the account of Noah and his family. Noah was a righteous man, the only blameless person living on earth at the time, and he walked in close fellowship with God. Noah was the father of three sons: Shem, Ham and Japheth. Now God saw that the earth had become corrupt and was filled with violence. God observed all this corruption in the world, for everyone on earth was corrupt. So God said to Noah...

God   I have decided to destroy all living creatures, for they have filled the earth with violence. Yes, I will wipe them all out along with the earth! Build a large boat from cypress wood and waterproof it with tar, inside and out. Then construct decks and stalls throughout its interior. Make the boat 450 feet long, 75 feet wide, and 45 feet high. Leave an 18-inch opening below the roof all the way around the boat. Put the door on the side, and build three decks inside the boat—lower, middle, and upper. Look! I am about to cover the earth with a flood that will destroy every living thing that breaths. Everything on earth will die. But I will confirm my covenant with you. So enter the boat—you and your wife and your sons and their wives. Bring a pair of every kind of animal—a male and a female—into the boat with you to keep them alive during the flood. Pairs of every kind of bird, and every kind of animal, and every kind of small animal that scurries along the ground, will come to you to be kept alive. And be sure to take on board enough food for your family and for all the animals.

Narrator   So Noah did everything exactly as God had commanded him.
             When everything was ready, the Lord said to Noah...

God   Go into the boat with all your family, for among all the people of the earth, I can see that you alone are righteous. Take with you seven pairs -- male and female -- of each animal I have approved for eating and for sacrifice, and take one pair of each of the others. Also take seven pairs of every kind of bird. There must be a male and a female in each pair to ensure that all life will survive on the earth after the flood. Seven days from now I will make the rains pour down on the earth. And it will rain for forty days and forty nights, until I have wiped from the earth all the living things I have created.

Narrator   So Noah did everything as the Lord commanded him. Noah was 600 years old when the flood covered the earth. He went on board the boat as escape the

9

flood—he and his wife and his sons and their wives. With them were all the various kinds of animals—those approved for eating and for sacrifice and those that were not—along with all the birds and the small animals that scurry along the ground. They entered the boat in pairs, male and female, just as God had commanded Noah. After seven days, the waters of the flood came and covered the earth. When Noah was 600 years old, on the seventeenth day of the second month, all the underground waters erupted from the earth, and the rain fell in mighty torrents from the sky. The rain continued to fall for forty days and forty nights. That very day Noah had gone into the boat with his wife and his sons—Shem, Ham, and Japheth—and their wives. With them in the boat were pairs of every kind of animal—domestic and wild, large and small—along with birds of every kind. Two by two they came into the boat, representing every living thing that breathes. A male and female of each kind entered, just as God had commanded Noah. Then the Lord closed the door behind them. For forty days the floodwaters grew deeper, covering the ground and lifting the boat high above the earth. As the waters rose higher and higher above the ground, the boat floated safely on the surface. Finally, the water covered even the highest mountains on the earth, rising more than twenty-two feet above the highest peaks. All the living things on earth died—birds, domestic animals, wild animals, small animals that scurry along the ground, and all the people. Everything that breathed and lived on dry land died. God wiped out every living thing on the earth—people, livestock, small animals that scurry along the ground, and the birds of the sky. All were destroyed. The only people who survived were Noah and those with him in the boat. And the floodwaters covered the earth for 150 days. But God remembered Noah and all the wild animals and livestock with him in the boat. He sent a wind to blow across the earth, and the floodwaters began to recede. The underground waters stopped flowing, and the torrential rains from the sky were stopped. So the floodwaters gradually receded from the earth. After 150 days, exactly five months from the time the flood began, the boat came to rest on the mountain of Ararat. Two and a half months later, as the waters continues to go down, other mountain peaks became visible. After another forty days, Noah opened the window he had made in the boat and released a raven. The bird flew back and forth until the floodwaters on the earth had dried up. He also released a dove to see if the water had receded and it could find dry ground. But the dove could find no place to land because the water sill covered the ground. So it returned to the boat, and Noah held out his hand and drew the dove back inside. After waiting another seven days, Noah released the dove again. This time the dove returned to him in the evening with a fresh olive leaf in its beak. Then Noah knew that the floodwaters were almost gone. He waited another seven days and then released the dove again. This time it did not come back. Noah was now 601 years old. On the first day of the new year, ten and half months after the flood began, the floodwaters had almost dried up from the earth. Noah lifted back the covering of the boat and saw that the surface of the ground was drying. Two more months went by, and at last the earth was dry! Then God said to Noah...

God   Leave the boat, all of you—you and your wife, and the sons and their wives. Release all the animals—the birds, the livestock, and the small animals that scurry along the ground—so they can be fruitful and multiply throughout the earth.

Narrator   So Noah, his wife, and his sons and their wives left the boat. And all of the large and small animals and birds came out of the boat, pair by pair. Then Noah built an altar to the Lord, and there he sacrificed as burnt offerings the animals and birds that had been approved for that purpose. And the Lord was pleased with the aroma of the sacrifice and said to himself...

God   I will never again curse the ground because of the human race, even though everything they think or imagine is bent toward evil from childhood. I will never again destroy all living things. As long as the earth remains, there will be planting and harvest, cold and heat, summer and winter, day and night.

Narrator   Then God blessed Noah and his sons and told them...

God   Be fruitful and multiply. Fill the earth. All the animals of the earth, all the birds of the sky, all the small animals that scurry along the ground, and all the fish in the sea will look on you with fear and terror. I have placed them in your power. I have given them to you for food, just as I have given you grain and vegetables. But you must never eat any meat that still has the lifeblood in it. And I will require the blood of anyone who takes another person's life. If a wild animal kills a person, it must die. And anyone who murders a fellow human must die. If anyone takes a human life, that person's life will also be taken by human hands. For God made human beings in his own image. Now be fruitful and multiply, and repopulate the earth.

Narrator   Then God told Noah and his sons...

God   I hereby confirm my covenant with you and your descendants, and with all the animals that were on the boat with you—the birds, the livestock, and all the wild animals—every living creature on earth. Yes, I am confirming my covenant with you. Never again will floodwaters kill all living creatures; never again will a flood destroy the earth. I am giving you a sign of my covenant with you and with all living creatures, for all generations to come. I have placed my rainbow in the clouds. It is the sign of my covenant with you and with all the earth. When I send clouds over the earth, the rainbow will appear in the clouds, and I will remember my covenant with you and with all living creatures. Never again will the flood waters destroy all life.

The Call of Abram

Genesis 12, 13, 15:1-18 (NIV)

You will need:

Actors   Props

    Narrator   Altar

    Lord   Tent

    Abram   Stuffed Animals

    Pharaoh   Gold

    Lot (non–speaking)   Silver

    Sarai (non–speaking)   Pot

Tips:

- Create an altar by stacking shoe boxes.
- Use a sheet over a small table or chair to create a tent.
- Use old jewelry for gold and silver.
- Use pictures of animals if stuffed animals are not available.
- Place signs along the "path of travel" to designate the many places that get visited in this story: Harran, Canaan, Shechem, Bethel, Ai, Negev, Egypt, Sodom, and Hebron.

Set the scene:

Many people were sinning against God, but Abram and a few others were trying to follow Him. On several remarkable occasions, God spoke directly to Abram whose name was later changed to Abraham.

Discussion ideas:

- God asked Abram to leave his home and go to a land that he would show him. Would it be hard for you to move to a foreign country? What if you didn't even know where you would be going?

- God promised to bless Abram, but Abram had to do something pretty difficult first. Have you ever been asked to do something that was difficult? How did you handle it?
- Lot chose the best land for himself without thinking of Abram's needs or what would be fair. If you are splitting something with a friend, would you choose the biggest/best portion for yourself or allow your friend to choose a portion first?

Narrator   The Lord had said to Abram...

Lord   Go from your country, your people and your father's household to the land I will show you. I will make you into a great nation, and I will bless you; I will make your name great, and you will be a blessing. I will bless those who bless you, and whoever curses you I will curse; and all peoples on earth will be blessed through you.

Narrator   So Abram went, as the Lord had told him; and Lot went with him. Abram was seventy-five years old when he set out from Harran. He took his wife Sarai, his nephew Lot, all the possessions they had accumulated and the people they had acquired in Harran, and they set out for the land of Canaan, and they arrived there. Abram traveled through the land as far as the site of the great tree of Moreh at Shechem. At that time the Canaanites were in the land. The Lord appeared to Abram and said...

Lord   To your offspring I will give this land.

Narrator   So he built an altar there to the Lord, who had appeared to him. From there he went on toward the hills east of Bethel and pitched his tent, with Bethel on the west and Ai on the east. There he built an alter to the Lord and called on the name of the Lord. Then Abram set out and continued toward the Negev. Now there was a famine, in the land, and Abram went down to Egypt to live there for a while because the famine was severe. As he was about to enter Egypt, he said to his wife Sarai...

Abram   I know what a beautiful woman you are. When the Egyptians see you, they will say, 'This is his wife.' Then they will kill me but will let you live. Say you are my sister, so that I will be treated well for your sake and my life will be spared because of you.

Narrator   When Abram came to Egypt, the Egyptians saw that Sarai was a very beautiful woman. And when Pharaoh's officials saw her, they praised her to Pharaoh, and she was taken into his palace. He treated Abram well for her sake, and Abram acquired sheep and cattle, male and female donkeys, male and female servants, and camels. But the Lord inflected serious diseases on Pharaoh and his household because of Abram's wife Sarai. So Pharaoh summoned Abram.

Pharaoh   What have you done to me? Why didn't you tell me she was your wife? Why did you say, 'She is my sister,' so that I took her to be my wife? Now then, here is your wife. Take her and go!

Narrator   Then Pharaoh gave orders about Abram to his men, and they sent him on his way, with his wife and everything he had. So Abram went up from Egypt to the Negev, with his wife and everything he had, and Lot went with him. Abram had become very wealthy in livestock and in silver and gold. From the Negev he went from place to place until he came to Bethel, to the place between Bethel and Ai where his tent had been earlier and where he had first built on altar. There Abram called on the name of the Lord. Now Lot, who was moving about with Abram, also had flocks and herds and tents. But the land could not support them while they stayed together, for their possessions were so great that they were not able to stay together. And quarreling arose between Abram's herders and lot's. The Canaanites and Perizzites were also living in the land at that time. So Abram said to Lot...

Abram   Let's not have any quarreling between you and me, or between your herders and mine, for we are close relatives. Is not the whole land before you? Let's part company. If you go to the left, I'll go to the right; if you go the right, I'll go to the left.

Narrator   Lot looked around and saw that the whole plain of the Jordan toward Zoar was well watered, like the land of Egypt. (This was before the Lord destroyed Sodom and Gomorrah.) So Lot chose for himself the whole plain of the Jordan and set out toward the east. The two men parted company: Abram lived in the land of Canaan, while Lot lived among the cities of the plain and pitched his tents near Sodom. Now the people of Sodom were wicked and were sinning greatly against the Lord. The Lord said to Abram after Lot had parted from him...

Lord   Look around from where you are, to the north and south, to the east and west. All the land that you see I will give to you and your offspring forever. I will make your offspring like the dust of the earth, so that if anyone could count the dust, then your offspring could be counted. Go, walk through the length and breadth of the land, for I am giving it to you.

Narrator	So Abram went to live near the great trees of Mamre at Hebron, where he pitched his tents. There he built an altar to the Lord. The word of the Lord came to Abram in a vision:
Lord	Do not be afraid, Abram. I am your shield, your very great reward.
Abram	Sovereign Lord, what can you give me since I remain childless and the one who will inherit my estate is Eliezer of Damascus? You have given me no children; so a servant in my household will be my heir.
Lord	This man will not be your heir, but a son who is your own flesh and blood will be your heir.
Narrator	He took him outside and said...
Lord	Look up at the sky and count the stars—if indeed you can count them. So shall your offspring be.
Narrator	Abram believed the Lord, and he credited it to him as righteousness.
Lord	I am the Lord, who brought you out of Ur of the Chaldeans to give you this land to take possession of it.
Abram	Sovereign Lord, how can I know that I will gain possession of it?
Lord	Bring me a heifer, a goat and a ram, each three years old, along with a dove and a young pigeon.
Narrator	Abram brought all these to him, cut them in two and arranged the halves opposite each other; the birds, however, he did not cut in half. Then birds of prey came down on the carcasses, but Abram drove them away. As the sun was setting, Abram fell into a deep sleep, and a thick and dreadful darkness came over him. Then the Lord said to him...

Lord   Know for certain that for four hundred years your descendants will be strangers in a country not their own and that they will be enslaved and mistreated there. But I will punish the nation they serve as slaves, and afterward they will come out with great possessions. You, however, will go to your ancestors in peace and be buried at a good old age. In the fourth generation your descendants will come back here, for the sin of the Amorites has not yet reached its full measure.

Narrator   When the sun had set and darkness had fallen, a smoking firepot with a blazing torch appeared and passed between the pieces. On that day the Lord made a covenant with Abram and said...

Lord   To your descendants I give this land, from the Wadi of Egypt to the great river, the Euphrates.

Hagar and Ishmael

Genesis 16:1-16 (NIV)

You will need:

Actors   Props

    Narrator   Baby (Ishmael)

    Abram   River/spring

    Sarai

    Hagar

    Angel

Tips:

- Note the mature content in this story and be sure your students are mature enough to participate.
- Have Hagar serve Sarai a drink to show that she is a maidservant. Than have Sarai move location to Abram before the dialog begins.
- Use a blue sheet to represent the river/spring

Set the scene:

Sarai wanted a child very badly, but she and Abram had not yet been able to have a child. According to custom at that time, a man could have a child with the servant and include that child in his household.

Discussion ideas:

- Have you ever tried to "help God" when you thought He couldn't possibly help you in the way you wanted? What was the result?
- God had promised Abram and Sarai that they would have a child. Their plan to "help God" showed their lack of faith that God would keep his promise. Often God's plans for our lives don't happen in the time frame that we expect or desire. We have to have patience and wait for God's perfect timing.

Narrator	Now Sarai, Abram's wife, had borne him no children. But she had an Egyptian slave named Hagar; so she said to Abram...
Sarai	The LORD has kept me from having children. Go, sleep with my slave; perhaps I can build a family through her.
Narrator	Abram agrees to what Sarai said. So after Abram had been living in Canaan ten years, Sarai his wife took her Egyptian slave Hagar and gave her to her husband to be his wife. He slept with Hagar, and she conceived. When she knew she was pregnant, she began to despise her mistress. Then Sarai said to Abram...
Sarai	You are responsible for the wrong I am suffering. I put my slave in your arms, and now that she knows she is pregnant, she despises me. May the LORD judge between you and me.
Abram	Your slave is in your hands. Do with her whatever you think best.
Narrator	Then Sarai mistreated Hagar; so she fled from her. The angel of the LORD found Hagar near a spring in the desert; it was the spring that is beside the road to Shur. And he said...
Angel	Hagar, slave of Sarai, where have you come from and where are you going?
Hagar	I'm running away from my mistress Sarai.
Angel	Go back to your mistress and submit to her. I will increase your descendants so much that they will be too numerous to count. You are now pregnant and you will give birth to a son. You shall name him Ishmael, for the LORD has heard of your misery. He will be a wild donkey of a man; his hand will be against everyone and everyone's hand against him, and he will live in hostility toward all his brothers.
Narrator	She gave this name to the LORD who spoke to her...

Hagar   You are the God who sees me. I have now seen the One who sees me. That is why the well was called Beer Lahai Roi, it is still there, between Kadesh and Bered.

Narrator So Hagar bore Abram a son, and Abram gave the name Ishmael to the son she had borne. Abram was eighty-six years old when Hagar bore him Ishmael.

Abraham and Sarah

Genesis 18: 1-15, 21: 1-7 (ESV)

You will need:

Actors   Props

    Narrator   Bread

    Abraham   Table

    Sarah   Tent

    Lord   Baby (Isaac)

    Man

    2 Men (no- speaking)

Tips:

- Use toy food or pictures if bread is not available.
- Dim the lights between scenes to represent time passing.
- Place a sheet over a small table or chairs to create a tent.

Set the scene:

God has changed the names of Abram and Sarai to Abraham and Sarah. Abraham and Sarah are at home when visitors appear. It is customary to feed visitors and wash their feet because they have traveled a distance on foot.

Discussion Ideas:

- God had a plan for Abraham and Sarah and he was faithful to them even though it was in a different time frame than they wanted. Can you think of a time when you were asked to be patient and wait for an answer?
- Can you think of a time when you were asked to wait for something from someone and time seemed so slow?

- Is anything too hard for God? Abraham and Sarah were much too old to have children, yet God fulfilled his promise and gave them a child. Have you seen or heard about God doing something that seemed impossible? How about someone being healed after the doctors said they would probably never get better?

Narrator	And the Lord appeared to him by the oaks of Mamre, as he sat at the door of his tent in the heat of the day. He lifted up his eyes and looked, and behold, three men were standing in front of him. When he saw them, he ran from the tent door to meet them and bowed himself to the earth and said...
Abraham	O Lord, If I have found favor in your sight, do not pass by your servant. Let a little water be brought, and wash your feet, and rest yourselves under the tree, while I bring a morsel of bread, that you may refresh yourselves, and after that you may pass on—since you have come to your servant. So they said...
Man	Do as you have said.
Narrator	And Abraham went quickly into the tent to Sarah and said.
Abraham	Quick! Three seahs of fine flour! Knead it, and make cakes.
Narrator	And Abraham ran to the herd and took a calf, tender and good, and gave it to a young man, who prepared it quickly. Then he took curds and milk and the calf that he had prepared, and set it before them. And he stood by them under the tree while they ate.
Man	Where is Sarah your wife?
Abraham	She is in the tent.
Lord	I will surely return to you about this time next year, and Sarah your wife shall have a son.
Narrator	Sarah was listening at the tent door behind him. Now Abraham and Sarah were old, advanced in years. The way of women had ceased to be with Sarah. So Sarah laughed to herself.
Sarah	After I am worn out, and my lord is old, shall I have pleasure?

Lord   Why did Sarah laugh and say, 'Shall I indeed bear a child, now that I am old? Is anything too hard for the Lord? At the appointed time I will return to you, about this time next year, and Sarah shall have a son.

Narrator   But Sarah denied it.

Sarah   I did not laugh.

Lord   No, but you did laugh.

Narrator   The Lord visited Sarah as he had said, and the Lord did to Sarah as he had promised. And Sarah conceived and bore Abraham a son in his old age at the time of which God had spoken to him. Abraham called the name of his son who was born to him, who Sarah bore him, Isaac. And Abraham circumcised his son Isaac when he was eight days old, as God had commanded him. Abraham was a hundred years old when his son Isaac was born to him and Sarah said...

Sarah   God has made laughter for me; everyone who hears will laugh over me. Who would have said to Abraham that Sarah would nurse children? Yet I have born him a son in his old age.

Abraham Pleads for Sodom

Genesis 18: 16 - 19:29 (ESV)

You will need:

Actors   Props
    Narrator   Bread
    Lord
    Abraham
    Lot
    2 Angels (men)
    Men of Sodom (one speaking)
    2 Daughters (non-speaking)
    2 Sons-in-law (non-speaking)

Tips:

- Note the controversial topic in this story and be sure your students are mature enough to participate.
- Designate an area for Lot's house in Sodom and an area for the Abraham in Hebron.
- Let a student with outstretched arms represent the door.

Set the scene:

When Lot and Abraham separated, Lot chose to go to Sodom since the land looked best and Abraham went to Hebron. Sodom was a wicked place. The people of this town saw the coming of strangers as a chance for perverted and homosexual acts.

Discussion ideas:

- Sodom was a wicked place. Sexual violence was not the town's only problem. They were arrogant, unconcerned, and did not help the poor and needy. What was God's plan to deal with Sodom and their wickedness? Do you think God is pleased with our country today?

- Before destroying Sodom, God showed mercy on Lot and provided a way for him to escape the destruction. God shows mercy to all of us when we sin as well.

- Abraham pleaded with the Lord to save Lot. He interceded on Lot's behalf. We have the privilege of intercessory prayer today. We often pray for our friends and family when they are sick or going through a difficult situation. How does it make you feel to think that other people are praying for you?

Narrator	Then the men set out from there, and they looked down toward Sodom. And Abraham went with them to set them on their way. The Lord said...
Lord	Shall I hide from Abraham what I am about to do, seeing that Abraham shall surely become a great and mighty nation, and all the nations of the earth shall be blessed in him? For I have chosen him, that he may command his children and his household after him to keep the way of the Lord by doing righteousness and justice, so that the Lord may bring to Abraham what he has promised him. Because the outcry against Sodom and Gomorrah is great and their sin is very grave, I will go down to see whether they have done altogether according to the outcry that has come to me. And if not, I will know.
Narrator	So the men turned from there and went toward Sodom, but Abraham still stood before the Lord. Then Abraham drew near and said...
Abraham	Will you indeed sweep away the righteous with the wicked? Suppose there are fifty righteous within the city. Will you then sweep away the place and not spare it for the fifty righteous who are in it? Far be it from you to do such a thing, to put the righteous to death with the wicked, so that the righteous fare as the wicked! Far be that from you! Shall not the Judge of all the earth do what is just?
Lord	If I find at Sodom fifty righteous in the city, I will spare the whole place for their sake.
Abraham	Behold, I have undertaken to speak to the Lord, I who am but dust and ashes. Suppose five of the fifty righteous are lacking. Will you destroy the whole city for lack of five?
Lord	I will not destroy it if I find forty-five there.
Abraham	Suppose forty are found there.
Lord	For the sake of forty, I will not do it.
Abraham	Oh let not the Lord be angry, and I will speak. Suppose thirty are found there.

Lord	I will not do it, if I find thirty there.
Abraham	Behold, I have undertaken to speak to the Lord. Suppose twenty are found there.
Lord	For the sake of twenty I will not destroy it.
Abraham	Oh let not the Lord be angry, and I will speak again but this once. Suppose ten are found there.
Lord	For the sake of ten I will not destroy it.
Narrator	And the Lord went his way, when he had finished speaking to Abraham and Abraham returned to his place. The two angels came to Sodom in the evening, and Lot was sitting in the gate of Sodom. When Lot saw them, he rose to meet them and bowed himself with his face to the earth and said...
Lot	My lords, please turn aside to your servant's house and spend the night and wash your feet. Then you may rise up early and go on your way.
Men	No; we will spend the night in the town square.
Narrator	But he pressed them strongly; so they turned aside to him and entered his house. And he made them a feast and baked unleavened bread, and they ate. But before they lay down, the men of the city, the men of Sodom, both young and old, all the people to the last man, surrounded the house. And they called to Lot.
Men	Where are the men who came to you tonight? Bring them out to us, that we may know them.
Narrator	Lot went out to the men at the entrance, shut the door after him, and said...
Lot	I beg you, my brother, do not act so wickedly. Behold, I have two daughters who have not known any man. Let me bring them out to you, and do to them

as you please. Only do nothing to these men, for they have come under the shelter of my roof.

Men   Stand back! This fellow came to sojourn, and he has become the judge! Now we will deal worse with you than with them.

Narrator   Then they pressed hard against the man Lot, and drew near to break the door down. But the men reached out their hands and brought Lot into the house with them and shut the door. And they struck with blindness the men who were at the entrance of the house, both small and great, so that they wore themselves out groping at the door.

Men   Have you anyone else here? Son-in-law, sons, daughters, or anyone you have in the city, bring them out of the place. For we are about to destroy this place, because the outcry against its people has become great before the Lord, and the Lord has sent us to destroy it.

Narrator   So Lot went out and said to his sons-in-law, who were to marry his daughters.

Lot   Up! Get out of this place, for the Lord is about to destroy the city.

Narrator   But he seemed to his sons-in-law to be jesting. As morning dawned, the angels urged Lot, saying...

Angel   Up! Take your wife and your two daughters who are here, lest you be swept away in the punishment of the city.

Narrator   But he lingered. So the men seized him and his wife and his two daughters by the hand, the Lord being merciful to him, and they brought him out and set him outside the city. And as they brought them out, one said...

Angel   Escape for your life. Do not look back or stop anywhere in the valley. Escape to the hills, lest you be swept away.

Lot   Oh, no, my lords. Behold, your servant has found favor in your sight, and you have shown me great kindness in saving my life. But I cannot escape to the hills, lest the disaster overtake me and I die. Behold, this city is near enough to flee to, and it is a little one. Let me escape thee—is it not a little one?—and my life will be saved!

Angel   Behold, I grant you this favor also, that I will not overthrow the city of which you have spoken. Escape there quickly, for I can do nothing till you arrive there.

Narrator   Therefore the name of the city was called "Zoar". The sun had risen on the earth when Lot came to Zoar. The Lord rained on Sodom and Gomorrah sulfur and fire from the Lord out of the heaven. And he overthrew those cities, and all the valley, and all the inhabitants of the cities, and what grew on the grown. But Lot's wife, behind him, looked back, and she became a pillar of salt. And Abraham went early in the morning to the place where he had stood before the Lord. And he looked down toward Sodom and Gomorrah and toward all the land of the valley, and he looked and, behold, the smoke of the land went up like the smoke of a furnace. So it was that, when God destroyed the cities of the valley, God remembered Abraham and sent Lot out of the midst of the overthrow when he overthrew the cities in which Lot had lived.

God Cares for Hagar and Ishmael

Genesis 21: 8-21 (ESV)

You will need:

Actors   Props

    Narrator   Bottle of Water

    Sarah   Bread

    God   Bush

    Hagar

    Angel

    Abraham (non-speaking)

    Ishmael (child, non-speaking)

Tips:

- A large plant can serve as the bush or cover a chair with a green sheet to represent one.
- Create an area for Abraham and Sarah's house and an area for the wilderness of Beersheba.
- Use a tan sheet to represent the wilderness of Beersheba, which is a desert.

Set the scene:

Isaac and Ishmael were Abraham's sons: Isaac by his wife, Sarah and Ishmael by the servant Hagar. God had promised Abraham and Sarah a child, but Sarah thought she was too old to conceive. She instructed Abraham to have a child by the maidservant. After the maidservant had Ishmael, Sarah became pregnant and had Isaac.

Discussion ideas:

- Hagar was sure that Ishmael would die because they were alone in the desert without any water. God caused her to see a well and sent an angel to encourage her. Have you ever been in a situation that you thought was hopeless? Does it help to know that God takes care of his people?

- Abraham was worried about sending his son away, but God told him to do so. He told Abraham that he would make a nation of Ishmael as well. God had a plan for both Isaac and Ishmael, and He has a plan for you. Like Abraham, we have to trust God and obey him even though we can't always know what the outcome will be.

Narrator	And the child grew and was weaned. And Abraham made a great feast on the day that Isaac was weaned. But Sarah saw the son of Hagar the Egyptian, whom she had born to Abraham, laughing. So she said to Abraham...
Sarah	Cast out this slave woman with her son, for the son of this slave woman shall not be your heir with my son Isaac.
Narrator	And the thing was very displeasing to Abraham on account of his sons. But God said to Abraham...
God	Be not displeased because of the boy and because of your slave woman. Whatever Sarah says to you, do as she tells you, for through Isaac shall your offspring be named. And I will make a nation of the son of the slave woman also, because he is your offspring.
Narrator	So Abraham rose early in the morning and took bread and a skin of water and gave it to Hagar, putting it on her shoulder, along with the child, and sent her away. And she departed and wandered in the wilderness of Beersheba. When the water in the skin was gone, she put the child under one of the bushes. Then she went and sat down opposite him a good way off, about the distance of a bowshot, for she said...
Hagar	Let me not look on the death of the child.
Narrator	And as she sat opposite him, she lifted up her voice and wept. And God heard the voice of the boy, and the angel of God called to Hagar from heaven and said to her...
Angel	What troubles you, Hagar? Fear not, for God has heard the voice of the boy where he is. Up! Lift up the boy, and hold him fast with your hand, for I will make him into a great nation.
Narrator	Then God opened her eyes, and she saw a well of water. And she went and filled the skin with water and gave the boy a drink. And God was with the boy, and he grew up. He lived in the wilderness and became an expert with the bow. He lived in the wilderness of Paran, and his mother took a wife for him from the land of Egypt.

Abraham is Tested

Genesis 22: 1-19 (ESV)

You will need:

Actors

- Narrator
- God
- Abraham
- Isaac
- Angel
- Two Men (non-speaking)

Props

- Wood
- Knife
- Altar
- Rope
- Stuffed animal (ram)
- Plant (if available)

Tips:

- Use a table for the altar so Isaac can lie on it. If you choose to use a rope to have Abraham bind Isaac, have him sit on the table first so the student doesn't have to be picked up after being tied.
- For safety, use a toy or plastic knife.
- Have a student put the stuffed animal in a plant at the appropriate time.

Set the scene:

Abraham and Sarah waited a long time for a son and loved him very much. At the time of this story, Isaac is about 13 years old and Abraham is about 113 year old.

Discussion ideas:

- Isaac was an obedient child. Can you imagine what he was feeling when he realized that his father was going to sacrifice him on the altar? If you were Isaac what do you think you would have done?

- This journey took about 3 days, around 50 miles, and all the while Abraham thought that he was taking his beloved son to be sacrificed. What a test! Have you ever felt like you were being tested by God? How? What did you do?
- Abraham trusted God and showed that he was willing to sacrifice something that he loved dearly in order to obey God. Because of his obedience, God promised to bless him and multiply his offspring. We know that God did, indeed, fulfill that promise.

Narrator	And after these things God tested Abraham and said to him...

God	Abraham!

Abraham	Here I am.

God	Take your son, your only son Isaac, whom you love, and go the land of Moriah, and offer him there as a burnt offering on one of the mountains of which I shall tell you.

Narrator	So Abraham rose early in the morning, saddled his donkey, and took two of his young men with him, and his son Isaac. And he cut the wood for the burnt offering and arose and went to the place of which God had told him. On the third day Abraham lifted up his eyes and saw the place from afar. Then Abraham said to his young men...

Abraham	Stay here with the donkey; I and the boy will go over there and worship and come again to you. And Abraham took the wood of the burnt offering and laid it on Isaac his son. And he took in his hand the fire and the knife. So they went both of them together. And Isaac said to his father Abraham...

Isaac	My father!

Abraham	Here I am, my son.

Isaac	Behold, the fire and the wood, but where is the lamb for a burnt offering?

Abraham	God will provide for himself the lamb for a burnt offering, my son.

Narrator	So they went both of them together. When they came to the place of which God had told him, Abraham built the altar there and added the wood in order and bound Isaac his son and laid him on the altar, on top of the wood. Then Abraham reached out his hand and took the knife to slaughter his son. But the angel of the Lord called to him for heaven and said...

Angel	Abraham, Abraham!

Abraham   Here I am.

Angel   Do not lay your hand on the boy or do anything to him, for now I know that you fear God, seeing you have not withheld your son, your only son, from me.

Narrator   And Abraham lifted up his eyes and looked, and behold, behind him was a ram, caught in a thicket by his horns. And Abraham went and took the ram and offered it up as a burnt offering instead of his son. So Abraham called the name of that place, "The Lord will provide"; as it is said to this day, On the mount of the Lord it shall be provided. And the angel of the Lord called to Abraham a second time from heaven and said...

Angel   By myself I have sworn, declares the Lord, because you have done this and have not withheld your son, your only son. I will surely bless you, and I will surely multiply your offspring as the stars of heaven and as the sand that is on the seashore. And your offspring shall possess the gate of his enemies, and in you offspring shall all the nations of the earth be blessed, because you have obeyed my voice. So Abraham returned to his young men, and they arose and went together to Beersheba. And Abraham lived at Beersheba.

Isaac Marries Rebekah

Genesis 24: 1-67 (TLB)

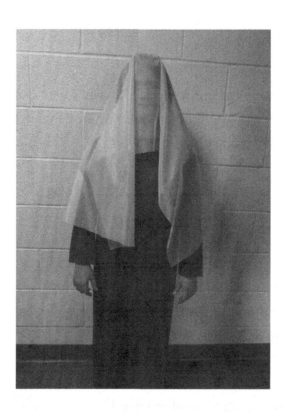

You will need:

Actors

    Narrator

    Abraham

    Servant

    Rebekah

    Laban (Rebekah's brother)

    Mother (Rebekah's)

    Betheul (Rebekah's father)

    Nurse (non-speaking)

Props

    Spring/Well

    Jar

    Jewelry

    Veil

Tips:

- Designate an area for well outside of the city, an area for Rebekah's house in Haran, and an area for Beerlahai-roi.

- Create a well by arranging chairs in a circle and wrapping it with a sheet.
- Instruct students to just pretend that there are camels, or allow 10 students to act as the camels. There were a few camel drivers travelling with the servant as well.

Set the scene:

It was customary for the parents of males to choose the mate for them and arrange the marriage. Abraham is living in Canaan, but his home country is Haran. Isaac is Abraham's beloved son.

Discussion ideas:

- Rebekah had a servant's heart. When the servant asked for water, she offered to get water for the camels too. Camels drink a lot of water and there were 10 of them. She would have had to fill her water jug many times in order to satisfy the camels. When she saw the need, she eagerly wanted to help out. Do you know anyone with a servant heart?
- Rebekah gave up a lot to leave her family and her own country to go and marry Isaac, whom she had never met. Have you ever been asked to leave your comfort zone and do something new?
- As soon as the servant realized that God had answered his prayer, he stopped and offered prayers of praise and thanksgiving. We need to remember to do the same when we see God answer prayers for us as well.

Narrator	Abraham was now a very old man, and God blessed him in every way. One day Abraham said to his household administrator, who was his oldest servant…
Abraham	Swear by Jehovah, the God of heaven and earth, that you will not let my son marry one of these local girls, these Canaanites. Go instead to my homeland, to my relatives, and find a wife for him there.
Servant	But suppose I can't find a girl who will come so far from home? Then shall I take Isaac there, to live among your relatives?
Abraham	No! Be careful that you don't do that under any circumstance. For the Lord God of heaven told me to leave that land and my people, and promised to give me and my children this land. He will send his angel on ahead of you, and he will see to it that you find a girl from there to be my son's wife. But if you don't succeed, then you are free from this oath; but under no circumstances are you to take my son there.
Narrator	So the servant vowed to follow Abraham's instructions. He took with him ten of Abraham's camels loaded with samples of the best of everything his master owned, and journeyed to Iraq, to Nahor's village. There he made the camels kneel down outside the town, beside a spring. It was evening, and the women of the village were coming to draw water.
Servant	[praying] O Jehovah, the God of my master, show kindness to my master Abraham and help me to accomplish the purpose of my journey. See, here I am, standing beside this spring, and the girls of the village are coming out to draw water. This is my request: When I ask one of them for a drink and she says, 'Yes, certainly, and I will water your camels too!'—let her be the one you have appointed as Isaac's wife. This is how I will know.
Narrator	As he was still speaking to the Lord about this, a beautiful young girl named Rebekah arrived with a water jug on her shoulder and filled it at the spring. (Her father was Bethuel the son of Nahor and his wife Milcah.) Running over to her the servant asked her for a drink.
Rebekah	[offer jug for him to drink] Certainly sir, I'll draw water for your camels, too, until they have enough!

Narrator	So she emptied the jug into the watering trough and ran down to the spring again and kept carrying water to the camels until they had enough. The servant said no more, but watched her carefully to see if she would finish the job, so that he would know whether she was the one. Then at last, when the camels had finished drinking, he produced a quarter-ounce gold earring and two five-ounce gold bracelets for her wrists.
Servant	Whose daughter are you, miss? Would your father have any room to put us up for the night?
Rebekah	My father is Bethuel. My grandparents are Milcah and Nahor. Yes, we have plenty of straw and food for the camels, and a guest room.
Narrator	The man stood there a moment with head bowed, worshiping Jehovah.
Servant	[praying] Thank you, Lord God of my master Abraham; thank you for being so kind and true to him, and for leading me straight to the family of my master's relatives.
Narrator	The girl ran home to tell her folks, and when her brother Laban saw the ring, and the bracelets on his sister's wrists, and heard her story, he rushed out to the spring where the man was still standing beside his camels, and said to him...
Laban	Come and stay with us, friend; why stand here outside the city when we have a room all ready for you, and a place prepared for the camels!
Narrator	So the man went home with Laban, and Laban gave him straw to bed down the camels, and feed for them, and water for the camel drivers to wash their feet. Then supper was served. But the old man said...
Servant	I don't want to eat until I have told you why I am here.
Laban	All right, tell us your errand.
Servant	I am Abraham's servant. And Jehovah has overwhelmed my master with blessings so that he is a great man among the people of his land. God has given him flocks of sheep and herds of cattle, and a fortune in silver and gold,

and many slaves and camels and donkeys. Now when Sarah, my master's wife, was very old, she gave birth to my master's son, and my master has given him everything he owns. And my master made me promise not to let Isaac marry one of the local girls, but to come to his relatives here in this far-off land, to his brother's family, and to bring back a girl from here to marry his son. 'But suppose I can't find a girl who will come?' I asked him. 'She will,' he told me— 'for my Lord, in whose presence I have walked, will send his angel with you and make your mission successful. Yes, find a girl among my relatives, from my brother's family. You are under oath to go and ask. If they won't send anyone, then you are freed from your promise.' Well, this afternoon when I came to the spring I prayed this prayer: 'O Jehovah, the God of my master Abraham, if you are planning to make my mission a success, please guide me in this way: Here I am, standing beside this spring. I will say to some girl who comes out to draw water, 'Please give me a drink of water!' And she will reply, 'Certainly! And I'll water your camels too!' Let that girl be the one you have selected to be the wife of my master's son.' Well, while I was still speaking these words, Rebekah was coming along with her water jug upon her shoulder; and she went down to the spring and drew water and filled the jug. I said to her, 'Please give me a drink.' She quickly lifted the jug down from her shoulder so that I could drink, and told me. 'Certainly, sir, and I will water your camels too!' So she did! Then I asked her, 'Whose family are you from?' And she told me, 'Nahor's. My father is Bethuel, the son of Nahor and his wife Milcah.' So I gave her the ring and the bracelets. Then I bowed my head and worshiped and blessed Jehovah, the God of my master Abraham, because he had led me along just the right path to find a girl from the family of my master's brother. So tell me, yes or no. Will you or won't you be kind to my master and do what is right? When you tell me, then I'll know what my next step should be, whether to move this way or that.

Bethuel   The Lord has obviously brought you here, so what can we say? Take her and go! Yes, let her be the wife of your master's son, as Jehovah has directed.

Narrator   At this reply Abraham's servant fell to his knees before Jehovah. Then he brought out jewels set in solid god and silver for Rebekah, and lovely clothing; and he gave may valuable presents to her mother and brother. Then they had supper, and the servant and the men with him stayed there overnight. But early the next morning he said...

Servant   Send me back to my master!

Mother   But we want Rebekah here at least another ten days or so! Then she can go.

Servant   Don't hinder my return: the Lord has made my mission successful, and I want to report back to my master.

Mother   Well, we'll call the girl and ask her what she thinks.

Narrator   So they called Rebekah.

Mother   Are you willing to go with this man?

Rebekah   Yes, I will go.

Narrator   So they told her good-bye, sending along the woman who had been her childhood nurse, and blessed her with this blessing as they parted.

Mother   Our sister, May you become the mother of many millions! May your descendants overcome all you enemies.

Narrator   So Rebekah and her servant girls mounted the camels and went with him. Meanwhile, Isaac, whose home was in the Negeb, had returned to Beerlahai-roi. One evening as he was taking a walk out in the fields, meditating, he looked up and saw the camels coming. Rebekah noticed him and quickly dismounted.

Rebekah   Who is that man walking through the field to meet us?

Servant   It is my master's son.

Narrator   So she covered her face with her veil. Then the servant told Isaac the whole story. And Isaac brought Rebekah into his mother's tent and she became his wife. He loved her very much, and she was a special comfort to him after the loss of his mother.

Isaac Blesses Jacob
Instead of Esau

Genesis 25: 27-34; 27: 1-40 (NET)

You will need:

Actors

    Narrator

    Esau

    Jacob

    Isaac

    Rebekah

Props

    Bowl and spoon

    Fur for hairy hand and neck

    Bow and Arrow (optional)

    Stuffed animals

    Shirt

Tips:

- Designate an area for Isaac's house. Within the house, designate a room for the kitchen and a separate room for Isaac. Also need an area near the house for the flock animals and an area further away for Esau to hunt game animals.
- Use a piece of cloth if fur is not available and wrap it around Jacob's forearms.
- Rebekah should instruct Jacob to put on the extra shirt and attach the fur before going in to see Isaac with the stew.
- If a toy bow and arrow are not available, have the students pretend.

Set the scene:

Isaac is very old and about to die. It was custom to give the birthright to the oldest son. Isaac had twin sons, Jacob and Esau. Esau was the oldest because he was born first.

Discussion ideas:

- Esau acted on impulse and traded the lasting benefits of his birthright for the immediate pleasure of food, without considering the future consequences. We can fall into this same trap. Have you ever acted suddenly and later regretted it?
- Rebekah took matters into her own hands and set out to trick her husband into giving the blessing to Jacob, even though God had already told her that Jacob would become the family leader. No matter how good our goals are, we should not try to achieve them by doing wrong. Can you think of a time when you were tempted to use deception to get what you wanted?

Narrator   When the boys grew up, Esau became a skilled hunter, a man of the open fields, but Jacob was an even-tempered man, living in tents. Isaac loved Esau because he had a taste for fresh game, but Rebecca loved Jacob. Now Jacob cooked some stew, and when Esau came in from the open fields, he was famished. So Esau said to Jacob...

Esau   Feed me some of the red stuff-yes, this red stuff-because I'm starving!

Narrator   (That is why he was also called Edom.)

Jacob   First sell me your birthright.

Esau   Look, I'm about to die! What use is the birthright to me?

Jacob   Swear an oath to me now.

Narrator   So Esau swore an oath to him and sold his birthright to Jacob. Then Jacob gave Esau some bread and lentil stew; Esau ate and drank, then got up and went out. So Esau despised his birthright. When Isaac was old and his eyes were so weak that he was almost blind, he called his older son Esau and said to him...

Isaac   My son.

Esau   Here I am

Isaac   Since I am so old, I could die at any time. Therefore, take your weapons-your quiver and your bow-and go out into the open fields and hunt down some wild game for me. Then prepare for me some tasty food, the kind I love, and bring it to me. Then I will eat it so that I may bless you before I die.

Narrator   Now Rebekah had been listening while Isaac spoke to his son Esau. When Esau went out to the open fields to hunt down some wild game and bring it back, Rebekah said to her son Jacob.

Rebekah   Look, I overheard your father tell your brother Esau, 'Bring me some wild game and prepare for me some tasty food. Then I will eat it and bless you in the presence of the Lord before I die.' Now then, my son, do exactly what I tell you! Go to the flock and get me two of the best young goats. I'll prepare them in a tasty way for your father, just the way he loves them. Then you will take it to your father. Thus he will eat it and bless you before he dies.

Jacob   But Esau my brother is a hairy man, and I have smooth skin! My father may touch me! Then he'll think I'm mocking him, and I'll bring a curse on myself instead of a blessing.

Rebekah   Any curse against you will fall on me, my son! Just obey me! Go and get them for me!

Narrator   So he went and got the goats and brought them to his mother. She prepared some tasty food, just the way his father loved it. Then Rebekah took her older son Esau's best clothes, which she had with her in the house, and put them on her younger son Jacob. She put the skins of the young goats on his hands and the smooth part of his neck. Then she handed the tasty food and the bread she had made to her son Jacob. He went to his father and said.

Jacob   My father.

Isaac   Here I am. Which are you, my son?

Jacob   I am Esau, your firstborn. I've done as you told me. Now sit up and eat some of my wild game so that you can bless me.

Isaac   How in the world did you find it so quickly, my son?

Jacob   Because the Lord your God brought it to me.

Isaac   Come closer so I can touch you, my son, and know for certain if you really are my son Esau.

Narrator   So Jacob went over to his father Isaac, who felt him and said.

Isaac   The voice is Jacob's, but the hands are Esau's

Narrator	He did not recognize him because his hands were hairy, like his brother Esau's hands. So Isaac blessed Jacob.
Isaac	Are you really my son Esau?
Jacob	I am.
Isaac	Bring some of the wild game for me to eat, my son. Then I will bless you.
Narrator	So Jacob brought it to him, and he ate it. He also bought him wine, and Isaac drank.
Isaac	Come hear and kiss me, my son.
Narrator	So Jacob went over and kissed him. When Isaac caught the scent of his clothing, he blessed him, saying...
Isaac	Yes, my son smells like the scent of an open field which the Lord has blessed. May God give you the dew of the sky and the richness of the earth, and plenty of grain and new wine. May peoples serve you and nations bow down to you. You will be lord over your brothers, and the sons of your mother will bow down to you. May those who curse you be cursed, and those who bless you be blessed.
Narrator	Isaac had just finished blessing Jacob, and Jacob had scarcely left his father's presence, when his brother Esau returned from the hunt. He also prepared some tasty food and brought it to his father.
Esau	My father, get up and eat some of your son's wild game. Then you can bless me.
Isaac	Who are you?
Esau	I am your firstborn son, Esau.
Narrator	Isaac began to shake violently and asked.

Isaac	Then who else hunted game and brought it to me? I ate all of it just before you arrived, and I blessed him. He will indeed be blessed!
Narrator	When Esau heard his father's words, he wailed loudly and bitterly. He said to his father...
Esau	Bless me too, my father!
Isaac	Your brother came in here deceitfully and took away your blessing.
Esau	Jacob is the right name for him! He has tripped me up two times! He took away my birthright, and now, look, he has taken away my blessing! Have you not kept back a blessing for me?
Isaac	Look! I have made him lord over you, I have made all his relatives his servants and provided him with grain and new wine. What is left that I can do for you, my son?
Esau	Do you have only that one blessing, my father? Bless me too!
Narrator	Then Esau wept loudly.
Isaac	Indeed, your home will be away from the richness of the earth, and away from the dew of the sky above. You will live by your sword but you will serve your brother. When you grow restless, you will tear off his yoke from your neck.

Joseph Sold by His Brothers

Genesis 37 (NET)

You will need:

Actors

      Narrator

      Jacob (Israel)

      Joseph

      Man

      Brothers (one speaking)

      Rueben (a brother)

      Judah (a brother)

      Ishmaelites (non-speaking)

      Potiphar (non-speaking)

Props

      Bright coat for Joseph

      Well / cistern

      20 shekels of silver

      Stuffed animal (goat)

      Sackcloth

Tips:

- Create an area for Jacob's home in Hebron, an area for a field in Shechem, an area with a well in Dothan, an area for Gilead, and an area for Egypt.
- Create a well by arranging chairs in a circle and wrapping it with sheets.
- Use a bright colorful bathrobe for the coat.
- Use coins for shekels.
- Use cloth for sackcloth. Wearing sackcloth was a sign of mourning, similar to us wearing black today.

Set the scene:

Jacob has 12 sons and they all are living with him.

Discussions Ideas:

- Could jealousy ever make you feel like hurting someone? Left unchecked, jealousy can grow quickly and lead to serious sins.

- Out of jealously, the brothers wanted to kill Jacob. Reuben saved Jacob's life by talking his brothers out of murder. Have you ever had to speak up among friends who are planning to do wrong? What happened?
- The brothers knew that killing their brother was wrong, so they sold him as a slave instead. When faced with a choice, be sure that you chose to do what is right and not just the lesser of two evils.

Narrator	But Jacob lived in the land where his father had stayed, in the land of Canaan. This is the account of Jacob. Joseph, his seventeen-year-old son, was taken care of the flocks with his brothers. Now he was a youngster working with the sons of Bilhah and Zilpah, his father's wives. Joseph brought back a bad report about them to their father. Now Israel loved Joseph more than all his sons because he was a son born to him late in life, and he made a special tunic for him. When Joseph's brothers saw that their father loved him more than any of them, they hated Joseph and were not able to speak to him kindly. Joseph had a dream, and when he told his brothers about it, they hated him even more. He said to them...
Joseph	Listen to this dream I had. There we were binding sheaves of grain in the middle of the field. Suddenly my sheaf rose up and stood upright and your sheaves surrounded my sheaf and bowed down to it!
Brothers	Do you really think you will rule over us or have dominion over us?
Narrator	They hated him even more because of his dream and because of what he said. Then he had another dream, and told it to his brothers.
Joseph	Look, I had another dream. The sun, the moon, and eleven stars were bowing down to me.
Narrator	When he told his father and his brothers, his father rebuked him, saying...
Jacob	What is this dream that you had? Will, I, your mother, and your brothers really come and bow down to you?
Narrator	His brothers were jealous of him, but his father kept in mind what Joseph said. When his brothers had gone to graze their father's flocks near Shechem, Israel said to Joseph.
Jacob	Your brothers are grazing the flocks near Shechem. Come, I will send you to them.
Joseph	I'm ready.

Jacob	Go now and check on the welfare of your brothers and of the flocks, and bring me word.
Narrator	So Jacob sent him from the valley of Hebron. When Joseph reached Shechem, a man found him wandering in the field, so the man asked him...
Man	What are you looking for?
Joseph	I'm looking for my brothers. Please tell me where they are grazing their flocks.
Man	They left this area, for I heard them say, 'Let's go to Dothan.'
Narrator	So Joseph went after his brothers and found them at Dothan. Now Joseph's brothers saw him from a distance, and before he reached them, they plotted to kill him. They said to one another...
Brothers	Here comes this master of dreams! Come now, let's kill him, throw him into one of the cisterns, and then say that a wild animal ate him. Then we'll see how his dreams turn out!
Narrator	When Reuben heard this, he rescued Joseph from their hands, saying...
Reuben	Let's not take his life! Don't shed blood! Throw him into this cistern that is here in the wilderness, but don't lay a hand on him.
Narrator	(Reuben said this, so he could rescue Joseph from them and take him back to his father) When Joseph reached his brothers, they stripped him of his tunic, the special tunic that he wore. Then they took him and threw him into the cistern. (Now the cistern was empty, there was no water in it. When they sat down to eat their food, they looked up and saw a caravan of Ishmaelites coming from Gilead. Their camels were carrying spices, balm, and myrrh down to Egypt. Then Judah said to his brothers...
Judah	What profit is there if we kill our brother and cover up his blood? Come, let's sell him to the Ishmaelites, but let's not lay a hand on him, for after all, he is brother, our own flesh.

Narrator	His brothers agreed. So when the Midianite merchants passed by, Joseph's brothers pulled him out of the cistern and sold him to the Ishmaelites for twenty pieces of silver. The Ishmaelites then took Joseph to Egypt. Later Reuben returned to the cistern to find that Joseph was not in it. He tore his clothes, returned to his brothers, and said...
Reuben	The boy isn't there! And I, where can I go?
Narrator	So they took Joseph's tunic, killed a young goat, and dipped the tunic in the blood. Then they brought the special tunic to their father and said...
Brothers	We found this. Determine now whether it is your son's tunic or not.
Narrator	He recognized it and exclaimed.
Jacob	It is my son's tunic. A wild animal has eaten him! Joseph has surely been torn to pieces!
Narrator	Then Jacob tore his clothes, put on sackcloth, and mourned for his son many days. All his sons and daughters stood by him to console him, but he refused to be consoled.
Jacob	No, I will go to the grave mourning my son.
Narrator	So Joseph's father wept for him. Now in Egypt the Midianites sold Joseph to Potiphar, one of Pharaoh's officials, the captain of the guard.

Pharaoh Puts Joseph in Charge

Genesis 39: 20-41:49 (ESV)

You will need:

Actors   Props

    Narrator   Prison with 3 places to sleep

    Joseph   Ring and gold chain

    Cupbearer   Robe

    Baker   Chariot

    Pharaoh

    Callers

    Joseph's Wife (non-speaking)

Tips:

- Put chairs together to make a chariot.
- Use a bathrobe or a coat for the robe.

Set the scene:

Joseph was put in charge of the house of Potiphar, one of Pharaoh's officials. Potiphar accused Joseph of making advances toward his wife, so he was sent to prison.

Discussion ideas:

- Joseph always gave God the credit for his abilities. We should be sure to do the same. Taking honor for ourselves instead of giving glory to God is a form of stealing God's honor. Can you think of a time when you did something great and had the opportunity to give God the glory?
- Joseph was both a prisoner and a slave in Egypt. He could have viewed his situation as hopeless and given up. But, he did not. He did his best with every task he was given and he was rewarded with favor from the prison wardens.

Have you ever found yourself in what seems like a hopeless situation? If you do, follow the example of Joseph and do your very best with even the small tasks. Your efforts will likely be rewarded as well.

- Joseph trusted God and was obedient. Pharaoh recognized that Joseph was a man of God and placed him in a position of power. You might not be asked to interpret dreams, but those you know should be able to see God in you. Do your family and friends see you as a Christian? How?

Narrator	And Joseph's master took him and put him into the prison, a place where the king's prisoners were confined, and he was there in prison. But the Lord was with Joseph and showed him steadfast love and gave him favor in the sight of the keeper of the prison. And the keeper of the prison put Joseph in charge of all the prisoners who were in the prison. Whatever was done there, he was the one who did it. The keeper of the prison paid no attention to anything that was in Joseph's charge, because the Lord was with him. And whatever he did, the Lord made it succeed. Sometime after this, the cupbearer of the king of Egypt and his baker committed an offense against their lord and king of Egypt. And Pharaoh was angry with his two officers, the chief cupbearer and the chief baker, and he put them in custody in the house of the captain of the guard, in the prison where Joseph was confined. The captain of the guard appointed Joseph to be with them, and he attended them. They continued for some time in custody. And one night they both dreamed—the cupbearer and the baker of the king of Egypt, Who were confined in the prison—each his own dream, and each dream with its own interpretation. When Joseph came to them in the morning, he saw that they were troubled. So he asked Pharaoh's officers who were with him in custody in his master's house...
Joseph	Why are your faces downcast today?
Baker	We have had dreams, and there is no one to interpret them.
Joseph	Do not interpretations belong to God? Please tell them to me.
Narrator	So the chief cupbearer told his dream to Joseph and said to him...
Cupbearer	In my dream there was a vine before me, and on the vine there were three branches. As soon as it budded, its blossoms shot forth, and the clusters ripened into grapes. Pharaoh's cup was in my hand, and I took the grapes and pressed them into Pharaoh's cup and placed the cup in Pharaoh's hand.
Joseph	This is its interpretation: The three branches are three days. In three days Pharaoh will lift up your head and restore you to your office, and you shall place Pharaoh's cup in his hand as formerly, when you were his cupbearer. Only remember me when it is well with you, and please do me the kindness

to mention me to Pharaoh, and so get me out of this house. For I was indeed stolen out of the land of the Hebrews, and here also I have done nothing that they should put me into the pit.

Narrator   When the chief baker saw that the interpretation was favorable, he said to Joseph...

Baker   I also had a dream; there were three cake baskets on my head, and in the uppermost basket there were all sorts of baked food for Pharaoh, but the birds were eating it out of the basket on my head.

Joseph   This is its interpretation: the three baskets are three days. In three days Pharaoh will lift up your head—from you!—and hang you on a tree. And the birds will eat the flesh from you.

Narrator   On the third day, which was Pharaoh's birthday, he made a feast for all his servants and lifted up the head of the chief cupbearer and the head of the chief baker among his servants. He restored the chief cupbearer to his position, and he placed the cup in Pharaoh's hand. But he hanged the chief baker, as Joseph had interpreted to them. Yet the chief cupbearer did not remember Joseph, but forgot him. After two whole years, Pharaoh dreamed that he was standing by the Nile, and behold, there came up out of the Nile seven cows attractive and plump, and they fed in the reed grass. And behold, seven other cows, ugly and thin, came up out of the Nile after them, and stood by the other cows on the bank of the Nile. And the ugly, thin cows ate up the seven attractive, plump cows. And Pharaoh awoke. And he fell asleep and dreamed a second time. And behold, seven ears of grain, plump and good, were growing on one stalk. And behold, after them sprouted seven ears, thin and blighted by the east wind. And the thin ears swallowed up the seven plump, full ears. And Pharaoh awoke, and behold, it was a dream. So in the morning his spirit was troubled, and he sent and called for all the magicians of Egypt and all its wise men. Pharaoh told them his dreams, but there was none who could interpret them to Pharaoh. Then the chief cupbearer said to Pharaoh...

Cupbearer I remember my offenses today. When Pharaoh was angry with his servants and put me and the chief baker in custody in the house of the captain of the guard, we dreamed on the same night, he and I, each having a dream with its own interpretation. A young Hebrew was there with us, a servant of the captain of the guard. When we told him, he interpreted our dreams to us, giving an interpretation to each man according to his dream. And as he interpreted to us, so it came about. I was restored to my office, and the baker was hanged.

Narrator   Then Pharaoh sent and called Joseph, and they quickly brought him out of the pit. And when he had shaved himself and changed his clothes, he came in before Pharaoh. And Pharaoh said to Joseph...

Pharaoh   I have had a dream, and there is no one who can interpret it. I have heard it said of you that when you hear a dream you can interpret it.

Joseph   It is not in me; God will give Pharaoh a favorable answer.

Narrator   Then Pharaoh said to Joseph...

Pharaoh   Behold, in my dream I was standing on the banks of the Nile. Seven cows, plump and attractive, came up out of the Nile and fed in the reed grass. Seven other cows came up after them, poor and very ugly and thin, such as I had never seen in all the land of Egypt. And the thin, ugly cows ate up the first seven plump cows, but when they had eaten them no one would have known that they had eaten them, for they were still as ugly as at the beginning. Then I awoke. I also saw in my dream seven ears growing on one stalk, full and good. Seven ears, withered, thin, and blighted by the east wind, sprouted after them, and the thin ears swallowed up the seven good ears. And I told it to the magicians, but there was no one who could explain it to me.

Joseph   The dreams of Pharaoh are one: God has revealed to Pharaoh what he is about to do. The seven good cows are seven years, and the seven good ears are seven years; the dreams are one. The seven lean and ugly cows that came up after them are seven years, and the seven empty ears blighted by the east wind are also seven years of famine. It is as I told Pharaoh: God has shown to Pharaoh what he is about to do. There will come seven years of great plenty throughout all the land of Egypt, but after them there will arise seven years of famine, and all the plenty will be forgotten in the land of Egypt. The famine will consume the land, and the plenty will be unknown in the land by reason of the famine that will follow, for it will be very severe. And the doubling of Pharaoh's dream means that the thing is fixed by God, and God will shortly bring it about. Now therefore let Pharaoh select a discerning and wise man, and set him over the land of Egypt. Let Pharaoh proceed to appoint overseers over the land and take one-fifth of the produce of the land of Egypt during the seven plentiful years. And let them gather all the food of these good years that are coming and store up grain under the authority of Pharaoh for food in the cities, and let them keep it. That food shall be a reserve for the land against the seven years of famine that are to occur in the land of Egypt, so that the land may not perish through the famine.

Narrator   This proposal pleased Pharaoh and all his servants. And Pharaoh said to his servants...

Pharaoh   Can we find a man like this, in whom is the Spirit of God?

Pharaoh   [turn to Joseph] Since God has shown you all this, there is none so discerning and wise as you are. You shall be over my house all people shall order themselves as you command. Only as regards the throne will I be greater than you. See, I have set you over all the land of Egypt.

Narrator   Then Pharaoh took his signet ring from his hand and put it on Joseph's hand, and clothed him in garments of fine linen and put a gold chain about his neck. And he made him ride in his second chariot. And they called out before him...

Callers   Bow the knee!

Narrator   Thus he set him over all the land of Egypt. Moreover, Pharaoh said to Joseph...

Pharaoh   I am Pharaoh, and without your consent no one shall lift up hand or foot in all the land of Egypt.

Narrator   And Pharaoh called Joseph's name Zaphenath-paneah. And he gave him in marriage Asenath, the daughter of Potiphera priest of On. So Joseph went out over the land of Egypt. Joseph was thirty years old when he entered the service of Pharaoh king of Egypt. And Joseph went out from the presence of Pharaoh and went through all the land of Egypt. During the seven plentiful years the earth produced abundantly, and he gathered up all the food of these seven years, which occurred in the land of Egypt, and put the food in the cities. He put in every city the food from the fields around it. And Joseph stored up grain in great abundance, like the sand of the sea, until he ceased to measure it, for it could not be measured.

Joseph's Brothers Go to Egypt

Genesis 42-45 (NLT)

You will need:

Actors

 Narrator
 Jacob (Israel)
 Joseph
 Brother
 Ruben
 Judah
 Pharaoh
 Manager
 Benjamin (non-speaking)
 Simeon (non-speaking)

Props

 Sacks (large-for grain)
 Cups
 Snacks of coins
 Rope (to tie Simeon)
 Donkeys (optional)
 Food (or basket)
 Gifts (see tips below)

Tips:

- Designate an area for Canaan and an area for Egypt.
- Use pillowcases filled with crumbled newspaper for large sacks of grain.
- The gifts consisted of balm, honey, gum, aromatic resin, pistachio nuts, and almonds. Use a few of these, whatever you have available.

Set the scene:

Joseph's brothers were jealous of him and sold him into slavery. Joseph interpreted dreams and warned Pharaoh about the coming famine. Joseph proved himself faithful and was put in charge of the whole land of Egypt.

Discussion ideas:

- Joseph's brothers wanted to get rid of him and sold him into slavery. But, God used the actions they meant to harm Joseph to make him prosper. God used

Joseph to eventually save the family that sent him away in the first place. God is sovereign and can turn even the worst situations into good. We can trust Him to take care of us! Can you think of a situation that seemed hopeless at the time, but God used it for your good later?

- Joseph forgave his brothers and shared his prosperity with them. Do you think that was difficult for him? Have you ever had to forgive someone that treated you badly?

Narrator	When Jacob heard that grain was available in Egypt, he said to his sons...
Jacob	Why are you standing around looking at one another? I have heard there is grain in Egypt. Go down there, and buy enough grain to keep us alive. Otherwise we'll die.
Narrator	So Joseph's ten older brothers went down to Egypt to buy grain. But Jacob wouldn't let Joseph's younger brother, Benjamin, go with them, for fear some harm might come to him. So Jacob's sons arrived in Egypt along with others to buy food, for the famine was in Canaan as well. Since Joseph was governor of all Egypt and in charge of selling grain to all the people, it was to him that his brothers came. When they arrived, they bowed before him with their faces to the ground. Joseph recognized his brothers instantly, but he pretended to be a stranger and spoke harshly to them.
Joseph	Where are you from?
Brother	From the land of Canaan. We have come to buy food.
Narrator	Although Joseph recognized his brother, they didn't recognize him. And he remembered the dreams he'd had about them many years before. He said to them...
Joseph	You are spies! You have come to see how vulnerable our land has become.
Brother	No, my lord! Your servants have simply come to buy food. We are all brothers – members of the same family. We are honest men, sir! We are not spies!
Joseph	Yes, you are! You have come to see how vulnerable our land has become.
Brother	Sir, there are actually twelve of us. We, your servants, are all brothers, sons of a man living in the land of Canaan. Our youngest brother is back there with our father right now, and one of our brothers is no longer with us.
Joseph	As I said, you are spies! This is how I will test your story. I swear by the life of Pharaoh that you will never leave Egypt unless your youngest brother comes

here! One of you must go and get your brother. I'll keep the rest of you here in prison. Then we'll find out whether or not your story is true. By the life of Pharaoh, if it turns out that you don't have a younger brother, then I'll know you are spies.

Narrator   So Joseph put them all in prison for three days. On the third day Joseph said to them...

Joseph   I am a God-fearing man. If you do as I say, you will live. If you really are honest men, choose one of your brothers to remain in prison. The rest of you may go home with grain for your starving families. But you must bring your youngest brother back to me. This will prove that your are telling the truth, and you will not die.

Narrator   To this they agreed. Speaking among themselves, they said...

Brother   Clearly we are being punished because of what we did to Joseph long ago. We saw his anguish when he pleaded for his life, but we wouldn't listen. That's why we're in this trouble.

Ruben   Didn't I tell you not to sin against the boy? But you wouldn't listen. And now we have to answer for his blood.

Narrator   Of course, they didn't know that Joseph understood them, for he had been speaking to them through an interpreter. Now he turned away from them and began to weep. When he regained his composure, he spoke to them again. Then he chose Simeon from among them and had him tied up right before their eyes. Joseph then ordered his servants to fill the men's sacks with grain, but he also gave secret instructions to return each brother's payment at the top of his sack. He also gave them supplies for their journey home. So the brothers loaded their donkeys with the grain and headed for home. But when they stopped for the night and one of them opened his sack to get grain for his donkey, he found his money in the top of his sack.

Brother   Look! My money has been returned; it's here in my sack!

Narrator   Then their hearts sank. Trembling, they said to each other...

Brother   What has God done to us?

Narrator   When the brothers came to their father, Jacob, in the land of Canaan, they told him everything that had happened to them.

Brother   The man who is governor of the land spoke very harshly to us. He accused us of being spies scouting the land. But we said, 'We are honest men, not spies. We are twelve brothers, sons of one father. One brother is no longer with us, and the youngest is at home with our father in the land of Canaan. Then the man who is governor of the land told us, 'This is how I will find out if you are honest men. Leave one of your brothers here with me, and take grain for your starving families and go on home. But you must bring your youngest brother back to me. Then I will know you are honest men and not spies. Then I will give you back your brother, and you may trade freely in the land.

Narrator   As they emptied out their sacks, there in each man's sack was the bag of money he had paid for the grain! The brothers and their father were terrified when they saw the bags of money.

Jacob   You are robbing me of my children! Joseph is gone! Simeon is gone! And now you want to take Benjamin, too. Everything is going against me!

Ruben   You may kill my two sons if I don't bring Benjamin back to you. I'll be responsible to him, and I promise to bring him back.

Jacob   My son will not go down with you. His brother Joseph is dead, and he is all I have left. If anything should happen to him on your journey, you would send this grieving, white-haired man to his grave.

Narrator   But the famine continued to ravage the land of Canaan. When the grain they had brought from Egypt was almost gone, Jacob said to his sons...

Jacob   Go back and buy us a little more food.

Judah	The man was serious when he warned us, 'You won't see my face again unless your brother is with you.' If you send Benjamin with us, we will go down and buy more food. But if you don't let Benjamin go, we won't go either. Remember, the man said, 'you won't see my face again unless your brother is with you.'
Jacob	Why were you so cruel to me? Why did you tell him you had another brother?
Brother	The man kept asking us questions about our family, 'Is your father still alive? Do you have another brother?' So we answered his questions. How could we know he would say, 'Bring your brother down here?'
Judah	Send the boy with me, and we will be on our way. Otherwise we will all die of starvation—and not only we, but you and our little ones. I personally guarantee his safety. You may hold me responsible if I don't bring him back to you. Then let me bear the blame forever. If we hadn't wasted all this time, we could have gone and returned twice by now.
Narrator	So their father, Jacob, finally said to them...
Jacob	If it can't be avoided, then at lease do this. Pack your bags with the best products of this land. Take them down to the man as gifts—balm, honey, gum, aromatic resin, pistachio nuts, and almonds. Also take double the money that was put back in your sacks, as it was probably someone's mistake. Then take your brother, and go back to the man. May God Almighty give you mercy as you go before the man, so that he will release Simeon and let Benjamin return. But if I must lose my children, so be it.
Narrator	So the men packed Jacob's gifts and double the money and headed off with Benjamin. They finally arrived in Egypt and presented themselves to Joseph. When Joseph saw Benjamin with them, he said to the manager of his household...
Joseph	These men will eat with me this noon. Take them inside the palace. Then go slaughter an animal, and prepare a big feast.

Narrator	So the man did as Joseph told him and took them into Joseph's palace. The Brothers were terrified when they saw that they were being taken into Joseph's house.
Brother	It's because of the money someone put in our sacks last time we were here. He plans to pretend that we stole it. Then he will seize us, make us slaves, and take our donkeys.
Narrator	The brothers approached the manager of Joseph's household and spoke to him at the entrance to the palace.
Brother	Sir, we came to Egypt once before to buy food. But as were returning home, we stopped for the night and opened our sacks. Then we discovered that each man's money—the exact amount paid—was in the top of his sack! Here it is; we have brought it back with us. We also have additional money to buy more food. We have no idea who put our money in our sacks.
Manager	Relax. Don't be afraid. Your God, the God of your father, must have put this treasure into your sacks. I know I received your payment.
Narrator	Then he released Simeon and brought him out to them. The manager then led the men into Joseph's palace. He gave them water to wash their feet and provided food for their donkeys. They were told they would be eating there, so they prepared their gifts for Joseph's arrival at noon. When Joseph came home, they gave him the gifts they had brought him, then bowed low to the ground before him. After greeting them, he asked...
Joseph	How is your father, the old man you spoke about? Is he still alive?
Brother	Yes, Our father, your servant, is alive and well.
Narrator	And they bowed low again. Then Joseph looked at his brother Benjamin, the son of his own mother.
Joseph	Is this your youngest brother, the one you told me about? May God be gracious to you, my son.

Narrator	The Joseph hurried from the room because he was overcome with emotion for his brother. He went into his private room, where he broke down and wept. After washing his face, he came back out, keeping himself under control. Then he ordered...
Joseph	Bring out the food.
Narrator	The waiters served Joseph at his own table, and his brother were served at a separate table. The Egyptians who were with Joseph sat at their own table, because Egyptians despised Hebrews and refuse to eat with them. Joseph told each of his brothers where to sit, and to their amazement, he seated them according to age, from oldest to youngest. And Joseph, filled their plates with food from his own table, giving Benjamin five times as much as he gave the others. So they feasted and drank freely with him. When his brothers were ready to leave, Joseph gave these instructions to his palace manager...
Joseph	Fill each of their sacks with as much grain as they can carry, and put each man's money back into his sack. Then put my personal silver cup at the top of the youngest brother's sack, along with the money for his grain.
Narrator	So the manager did as Joseph instructed him. The brothers were up at dawn and were sent on their journey with their loaded donkeys. But when they had gone only a short distance and were barely out of the city, Joseph said to his palace Manager.
Joseph	Chase after them and stop them. When you catch up with them, ask them, 'Why have you repaid my kindness with such evil? Why have you stolen my maker's silver cup, which he uses to predict the future? What a wicked thing you have done!
Narrator	When the palace manager caught up with the men, he spoke to them as he had been instructed.
Brothers	What you talking about? We are your servants and would never do such a thing! Didn't we return the money we found in our sacks? We brought it back all the way from the land of Canaan. Why would we steal silver or gold from

your master's house? If you find his cup with any one of us, let that man die. And all the rest of us, my lord, will be you salves.

Manager   That's fair. But only the one who stole the cup will be my slave. The rest of you may go free.

Narrator   They all quickly took their sacks from the backs of their donkeys and opened them. The palace manager searched the brother' sacks, from the oldest to the youngest. And the cup was found in Benjamin's sack! When the brothers saw this, they tore their clothing in despair. Then they loaded their donkeys again and returned to the city. Joseph was still in his palace when Judah and his brothers arrived, and they fell to the ground before him

Joseph   What have you done? Don't you know that a man like me can predict the future?

Judah   Oh, my lord, what can we say to you? How can we explain this? How can we prove our innocence? God is punishing us for our sins. My lord, we have all returned to be your slaves—all of us, not just our brother who had your cup in his sack.

Joseph   No, I would never do such a thing! Only the man who stole the cup will be my slave. The rest of you may go back to your father in peace.

Judah   [stepping toward Joseph] Please, my lord, let your servant say just one word to you. Please, do not be angry with me, even though you are as powerful as Pharaoh himself. My Lord, previously you asked us, your servants, 'Do you have a father or a brother'? And we responded, 'Yes, my lord, we have a father who is an old man, and his youngest son is a child of his old age. His full brother is dead, and he alone is left of his mother's children, and his father loves him very much. And you said to us, 'Bring him here so I can see him with my own eyes.' But we said to you, 'My lord, the boy cannot leave his father, for his father would die.' But you told us, 'Unless your youngest brother comes with you, you will never see my face again.' So we returned to your servant, our father, and told him what you had said. Later, when he said, 'Go back again and buy us more food,' we replied, 'We can't go unless you let our youngest brother go with us. We'll never get to see the man's face unless our youngest brother is with us.'

Then my father said to us, 'As you know, my wife had two sons, and one of them went away and never returned. Doubtless he was torn to pieces by some wild animal. I have never seen him since. Now if you take his brother away from me, and any harm comes to him, you will send this grieving, white-haired man to his grave.' And now, my lord, I cannot go back to my father without the boy. Our father's life is bound up in the boy's life. If he sees that the boy is not with us, our father will die. We, your servants, will indeed be responsible for sending that grieving, white-haired man to his grave. My lord, I guaranteed to my father that I would take care of the boy. I told him, 'If I don't bring him back to you, I will bear the blame forever. So please, my lord, let me stay here as a slave instead of the boy, and let the boy return with his brothers. For how can I return to my father if the boy is not with me? I couldn't bear to see the anguish this would cause my father!

Narrator   Joseph could stand it no longer. There were many people in the room, and he said to his attendants.

Joseph   Out, all of you!

Narrator   So he was alone with his brothers when he told them who he was. Then he broke down and wept. He wept so loudly the Egyptians could hear him, and word of it quickly carried to Pharaoh's palace.

Joseph   I am Joseph! Is my father still alive?

Narrator   But his brothers were speechless! They were stunned to realize that Joseph was standing there in front of them.

Joseph   Please, come closer.

Narrator   So they came closer. And he said again...

Joseph   I am Joseph, your brother, whom you sold into slavery in Egypt. But don't be upset, and don't be angry with yourselves for selling me to this place. It was God who sent me here ahead of you to preserve your lives. This famine that has ravaged the land for two years will last five more years, and there will be neither plowing nor harvesting. God has sent me ahead of you to keep you and your families alive and to preserve many survivors. So it was God who sent me here, not you! And he is the one who made me an adviser to Pharaoh—the manager of his entire palace and the governor of all Egypt. Now hurry back to my father and tell him, 'This is what you son Joseph says: God has made me master after all the land of Egypt. So come down to me immediately! You can live in the region of Goshen, where you can be near me with all you children and grandchildren, your flocks and herds, and everything you own. I will take care of you there, for there are still five years of famine ahead of us. Otherwise you, your household, and all your animals will starve. Look! You can see for yourselves, and so can my brother Benjamin, that I really am Joseph! Go tell my father of my honored position here in Egypt. Describe for him everything you have seen, and then bring my father here quickly.

Narrator   Weeping with joy, he embraced Benjamin, and Benjamin did the same. Then Joseph kissed each of his brothers and wept over them, and after that they began talking freely with him. The news soon reached Pharaoh's palace. Joseph's brothers have arrived! Pharaoh and his officials were all delighted to hear this.

Pharaoh   [to Joseph] Tell your brother, 'This is what you must do: Load your pack animals, and hurry back to the land of Canaan. Then get your father and all of your families, and return here to me. I will give you the very best land in Egypt, and you will eat from the best that the land produces. Tell your brothers, 'Take wagons from the land of Egypt to carry your little children and your wives, and bring your father here. Don't worry about your personal belonging, for the best of all the land of Egypt is yours.

Narrator   So the sons of Jacob did as they were told. Joseph provided them with wagons, as Pharaoh had commended, and he gave them supplies for the journey. And he gave each of them new clothes—but to Benjamin he gave five changes of clothes and 300 pieces of silver. He also sent his father ten male donkeys loaded with the finest products of Egypt, and ten female donkeys loaded with grain and bread and other supplies he would need on his journey. So Joseph sent his brothers off, and as they left, he called after them...

Joseph   Don't quarrel about all this along the way!

Narrator   And they left Egypt and returned to their father, Jacob, in the land of Canaan.

Brother   Joseph is still alive! And he is governor of all the land of Egypt!

Narrator   Jacob was stunned at the news—he couldn't believe it. But when they repeated to Jacob everything Joseph had told them, and when he saw the wagons Joseph had sent to carry him, their father's spirits revived. Then Jacob exclaimed...

Jacob   It must be true! My son Joseph is alive! I must go and see him before I die.

The Birth of Moses

Exodus 1: 1 – 2:10 (ESV)

You will need:

Actors

    Narrator
    Pharaoh
    Midwives (2)(one speaking)
    Daughter (Pharaoh's Daughter)
    Sister
    Child's mother (Levite woman)

Props

    Basket with a baby
    Reeds
    River

Tips:

- Use a blue sheet to create the river.
- Use a house plant to represent the reeds where the sister places the basket.

Set the scene:

Four hundred years have passed since Jacob moved his family to Egypt. These descendants of Abraham had grown to over two million strong. They were foreigners to the Egyptian Pharaoh and their growing numbers were becoming threatening.

Discussion ideas:

- The baby's mother was reunited with her baby. Out of desperation, she made a plan to save her baby. God used this mother to save that baby and ultimately that baby (Moses) will rescue God's people from Egypt. God can use the smallest acts to accomplish his great plan.
- Pharaoh's plan to kill all male babies was evil. Do you ever feel like everything is working against you and there is nothing you can do about it? When faced with evil, look for ways to act against it and trust God to use your effort.

Narrator   These are the names of the sons of Israel who came to Egypt with Jacob, each with his household: Reuben, Simeon, Levi, and Judah, Issachar, Zebulun, and Benjamin, Dan and Naphtali, Gad and Asher. All the descendants of Jacob were seventy persons; Joseph was already in Egypt. Then Joseph died, and all his brothers and all that generation. But the People of Israel were fruitful and increased greatly; they multiplied and grew exceedingly strong, so that the land was filled with them. Now there arose a new king over Egypt, who did not know Joseph. And he said to his people...

Pharaoh   Behold, the people of Israel are too many and too mighty for us. Come, let us deal shrewdly with them, lest they multiply, and, if war breaks out, they join our enemies and fight against us and escape from the land.

Narrator   Therefore they set taskmasters over them to afflict them with heavy burdens. They built for Pharaoh store cities, Pithom and Raamses. But the more they were oppressed, the more they multiplied and the more they spread abroad. And the Egyptians were in dread of the people of Israel. So they ruthlessly made the people of Israel work as slaves and made their lives bitter with hard service, in mortar and brick, and in all kinds of work in the field. In all their work they ruthlessly made them work as slaves. Then the king of Egypt said to the Hebrew midwives, one of whom was named Shiphrah and the other Puah.

Pharaoh   When you serve as midwife to the Hebrew women and see them on the birthstool, if it is a son, you shall kill him, but if it is a daughter, she shall live.

Narrator   But the midwives feared God and did not do as the king of Egypt, commanded them, but let the male children live. So the king of Egypt called the midwives and said to them...

Pharaoh   Why have you done this, and let the male children live?

Midwives   Because the Hebrew women are not like the Egyptian women, for they are vigorous and give birth before the midwife comes to them.

Narrator   So God dealt well with the midwives. And the people multiplied and grew very strong. And because the midwives feared God, he gave them families. Then Pharaoh commanded all his people...

Pharaoh   Every son that is born to the Hebrews you shall cast into the Nile, but you shall let every daughter live.

Narrator   Now a man from the house of Levi went and took as his wife a Levite woman. The woman conceived and bore a son, and when she saw that he was a fine child, she hid him three months. When she could hide him no longer, she took for him a basket made of bulrushes and daubed it with bitumen and pitch. She put the child in it and placed it among the reeds by the river bank. And his sister stood at a distance to know what would be done to him. Now the daughter of Pharaoh came down to bathe at the river, while her young women walked beside the river. She saw the basket among the reeds and sent her servant woman, and she took it. When she opened it, she saw the child, and behold, the baby was crying. She took pity on him and said...

Daughter   This is one of the Hebrews' children.

Narrator   Then his sister said to Pharaoh's daughter...

Sister   Shall I go and call you a nurse from the Hebrew women to nurse the child for you?

Narrator   And Pharaoh's daughter said to her...

Daughter   Go.

Narrator   So the girl went and called the child's mother. And Pharaoh's daughter said to her...

Daughter   Take this child away and nurse him for me, and I will give you your wages.

Narrator   So the woman took the child and nursed him. When the child grew older, she brought him to Pharaoh's daughter and he became her son. She named him Moses, she said...

Daughter   Because I drew him out of water.

Moses and the Burning Bush

Exodus 2: 11 – 3:20 (NET)

You will need:

Actors   Props

      Narrator   Bush

      God   Sandals (for Moses)

      Moses   Well

      Reuel

      Man

      Daughter

      Egyptian (non-speaking)

Tips:

- Designate an area for Midian with a well and an area for the desert with the bush.
- Create a well by arranging chairs in a circle and wrap with sheets.
- Use a large plant for the bush and shine a flashlight on it or add red and orange crepe paper to make the bush appear to be burning.

Set the scene:

The Hebrews have been slaves in Egypt for years.

Discussion ideas:

- Moses thought no one was watching when he killed the Egyptian. Sometimes we think we can get away with doing wrong if we don't get caught. However, our wrong doings will usually catch up with us.
- God spoke to Moses from a burning bush. Isn't that an unexpected source? God may use unexpected sources today as well – friends, parents, thoughts or

experiences. Can you think of a time when God spoke to you in an unexpected way? How?

- God chose Moses for a mighty task even after Moses had made some pretty big mistakes. If you ever feel like you have messed up too bad to be of any use to God, just remember Moses. God had a plan for Moses, and He has a plan for you as well.

Narrator	In those days, when Moses had grown up, he went out to his people and observed their hard labor, and he saw an Egyptian man attacking a Hebrew man, one of his own people. He looked this way and that and saw that no one was there, and then he attacked the Egyptian and concealed the body in the sand. When he went out the next day, there were two Hebrew men fighting. So he said to the one who was in the wrong...
Moses	Why are you attacking your fellow Hebrew?
Man	Who made you a ruler and a judge over us? Are you planning to kill me like you killed that Egyptian?
Narrator	Then Moses was afraid, thinking,
Moses	Surely what I did has become known.
Narrator	When Pharaoh heard about this event, he sought to kill Moses. So Moses fled from Pharaoh and settled in the land of Midian, and he settled by a certain well. Now a priest of Midian had seven daughters, and they came and began to draw water and fill the troughs in order to water their father's flock. When some shepherds came and drove them away, Moses came up and defended them and then watered their flock. So when they came home to their father Reuel, he asked...
Reuel	Why have you come home so early today?
Daughter	An Egyptian man rescued us from the shepherds, and he actually drew water for us and watered the flock!
Narrator	He said to his daughters...
Reuel	So where is he? Why in the world did you leave the man? Call him, so that he may eat a meal with us.
Narrator	Moses agreed to stay with the man, and he gave his daughter Zipporah to Moses in marriage. When she bore a son Moses named him Gershom, for he said...

Moses	I have become a resident foreigner in a foreign land.
Narrator	During that long period of time the king of Egypt died, and the Israelites groaned because of the slave labor. They cried out, and their desperate cry because of their slave labor went up to God. God heard their groaning, God remembered his covenant with Abraham, with Isaac, and with Jacob, God saw the Israelites, and God understood...Now Moses was shepherding the flock of his father-in-law Jethro, the priest of Midian, and he led the flock to the far side of the desert and came to the mountain of God, to Horeb. The angel of the Lord appeared to him in a flame of fire from within a bush. He looked-and the bush was ablaze with fire, but it was not being consumed! So Moses thought,
Moses	I will turn aside to see this amazing sight. Why does the bush not burn up?
Narrator	When the Lord saw that he had turned aside to look, God called to him from within the bush and said...
God	Moses, Moses!
Moses	Here I am.
God	Do not approach any closer! Take your sandals off your feet, for the place where you are standing is holy ground. I am the God of your father, the God of Abraham, the God o Isaac, and the God of Jacob.
Narrator	Then Moses hid his face, because he was afraid to look at God.
God	I have surely seen the affliction of my people who are in Egypt. I have heard their cry because of their taskmasters, for I know their sorrows. I have come down to deliver them from the hand of the Egyptians and to bring them up from that land to a land that is both good and spacious, to a land flowing with milk and honey, to the region of the Canaanites, Hittites, Amorites, Perizzites, Hivites, and Jebusites. And now indeed the cry of the Israelites has come to me, and I have also seen how severely the Egyptians oppress them. So now go, and I will send you to Pharaoh to bring my people, the Israelites, out of Egypt.

| Moses | Who am I, that I should go to Pharaoh, or that I should bring the Israelites out of Egypt? |

| God | Surely I will be with you, and this will be the sign to you that I have sent you: When you bring the people out of Egypt, you and they will serve God on this mountain. |

| Moses | If I go the Israelites and tell them, 'The God of your fathers has sent me to you,' and they ask me, 'What is his name?-what should I say to them? |

| God | I Am that I Am. You must say this to the Israelites, I Am has sent me to you. You must say this to the Israelites, The Lord-the God of your fathers, the God of Abraham, and the God of Isaac, and the God of Jacob-has sent me to you. This is my name forever, and this is my memorial from generation to generation. Go and bring together the elders of Israel and tell them, The Lord, the God of your fathers, appeared to me-the God of Abraham, Isaac, and Jacob-saying, I have attended carefully to you and to what has been done to you in Egypt, and I have promised that I will bring you up out of the affliction of Egypt to the land of the Canaanites, Hittites, Amorites, Perizzites, Hivites, and Jebusites, to a land flowing with milk and honey. The elders will listen to you, and then you and the elders of Israel must go to the king of Egypt and tell him, 'The Lord, the God of the Hebrews, has met with us. So now, let us go three days journey into the wilderness, so that we may sacrifice to the Lord our God.' But I know that the king of Egypt will not let you go, not even under force. So I will extend my hand and strike Egypt with all my wonders that I will do among them, and after that he will release you. |

Plagues Strike Egypt

Exodus 7: 14 – 10:29 (NET)

You will need:

Actors

    Narrator
    Lord
    Pharaoh
    Moses
    Magicians
    Servants
    Sorcerers (non-speaking)
    Officials (non-speaking)
    Aaron (non-speaking)

Props

    Staff
    Snakes
    Blood
    Water
    Frogs
    Lice
    Flies
    Livestock
    Boils
    Hail
    Locusts

Tips:

- Many of these props can be found at a "dollar" store. Here are a few ideas:

    Ping pong balls for hail,

Toy snakes, frogs and flies,
Small circular band-aids for the boils,
Red food coloring for turning water into blood.

Set the scene:

The Israelites were captives of Pharaoh in Egypt and were not able to worship God. They wanted to leave, but Pharaoh did not want them to go because they were the workforce in Egypt.

Discussion ideas:

- Pharaoh wanted a compromise (A settlement in which each side gives up some demands). He would allow the Hebrews to sacrifice to their God as long as they didn't go far away. Sometimes believers will be tempted to compromise and only be partially obedient to God's commands. Have you ever been in a situation like this? What did you do?

Narrator   The Lord said to Moses...

Lord   Pharaoh's heart is hard, he refuses to release the people. Go to Pharaoh in the morning when he goes out to water. Position yourself to meet him by the edge of the Nile, and take in your hand the staff that was turned into a snake. Tell him, The Lord, the God of the Hebrews, has sent me to you to say, Release my people, that they may serve me in the desert! But until now you have not listened. Thus says the Lord: By this you will know that I am the Lord: I am going to strike the water of the Nile with the staff that is in my hand, and it will be turned into blood. Fish in the Nile will die, the Nile will stink, and the Egyptians will be unable to drink water from the Nile. Tell Aaron, Take your staff and stretch out your hand over Egypt's waters-over their rivers, over their canals, over their ponds, and over all their reservoirs-so that it becomes blood. There will be blood everywhere in the land of Egypt, even in wooden and stone containers.

Narrator   Moses and Aaron did so, just as the Lord had commanded. Moses raised the staff and struck the water that was in the Nile right before the eyes of Pharaoh and his servants, and all the water that was in the Nile was turned to blood. When the fish that were in the Nile died, the Nile began to stink, so that the Egyptians could not drink water from the Nile. There was blood everywhere in the land of Egypt! But the magicians of Egypt did the same by their secret arts, and so Pharaoh's heart remained hard, and he refused to listen to Moses and Aaron-just as the Lord had predicted. And Pharaoh turned and went into his house. He did not pay any attention to this. All the Egyptians dug around the Nile for water to drink because they could not drink the water of the Nile. Seven full days passed after the Lord struck the Nile. Then the Lord said to Moses.

Lord   Go to Pharaoh and tell him, Thus says the Lord: Release my people in order that they may serve me! But if you refuse to release them, then I am going to plague all your territory with frogs. The Nile will swarm with frogs, and they will come up and go into your house, in your bedroom, and on your bed, and into the houses of your servants and your people, and into your ovens and your kneading troughs. Frogs will come up against you, your people, and all your servants. Tell Aaron, Extend your hand with your staff over the rivers, over the canals, and over the ponds, and bring the frogs up over the land of Egypt.

Narrator	So Aaron extended his hand over the waters of Egypt, and frogs came up and covered the land of Egypt. The magicians did the same with their secret arts and brought up frogs on the land of Egypt too. Then Pharaoh summoned Moses and Aaron and said...
Pharaoh	Pray to the Lord that He may take the frogs away from me and my people, and I will release the people that they may sacrifice to the Lord.
Moses	You may have the honor over me-when shall I pray for you, your servants, and your people, for the frogs to be removed from you and your houses, so that they will be left only in the Nile?
Pharaoh	Tomorrow.
Lord	Tell Aaron, extend your staff and strike the dust of the ground and it will become gnats throughout all the land of Egypt.
Narrator	They did so; Aaron extended his hand with his staff, he struck the dust of the ground, and it became gnats on people and on animals. All the dust of the ground became gnats throughout all the land of Egypt. When the magicians attempted to bring forth gnats by their secret arts, they could not. So there were gnats on people and on animals.
Magician	It is the finger of God!
Narrator	But Pharaoh's heart remained hard, and he did not listen to them just as the Lord had predicted.
Moses	It will be as you say, so that you may know that there is no one like the Lord our God. The frogs will depart from you, your houses, your servants, and your people; they will be left only in the Nile.
Narrator	Then Moses and Aaron went out from Pharaoh, and Moses cried to the Lord because of the frogs that he had brought on Pharaoh. The Lord did as Moses asked-the frogs died out of the houses, the villages, and the fields. The Egyptians piled them in countless heaps, and the land stank. But when Pharaoh saw that

there was relief, he hardened his heart and did not listen to them, just as the Lord had predicted.

Narrator   They did so; Aaron extended his hand with his staff, he struck the dust of the ground, and it became gnats on people and on animals. All the dust of the ground became gnats throughout all the land of Egypt. When the magicians attempted to bring forth gnats by their secret arts, they could not. So there were gnats on people and on animals. The Magicians said to Pharaoh.

Magicians   This is the finger of God.

Narrator   But Pharaoh's heart remained hard, and he did not listen to the, just as the Lord had predicted.

Lord   Get up early in the morning and position yourself before Pharaoh as he goes out to the water, and tell him. Thus says the Lord, Release my people that they may serve me! If you do not release my people, then I am going to send swarms of flies on you and on your servants and on your people and in your houses. The houses of the Egyptians will be full of flies, and even the ground they stand on. But on that day I will mark off the land of Goshen, where my people are staying so that no swarms of flies will be there, that you may know that I am the Lord in the midst of this land. I will put a division between my people and your people. This sign will take place tomorrow.

Narrator   The Lord did so; a thick swarm of flies came into Pharaoh's house and into the houses of his servants, and throughout the whole land of Egypt the land was ruined because of the swarms of flies. Then Pharaoh summoned Moses and Aaron and said...

Pharaoh   Go, sacrifice to your God within the land.

Moses   That would not be the right thing to do, for the sacrifices we make to the Lord our God would be an abomination to the Egyptians. If we make sacrifices that are on abomination to the Egyptians right before their eyes, will they not stone us? We must go on a three-day journey into the desert and sacrifice to the Lord our God, just as he is telling us.

Pharaoh   I will release you so that you may sacrifice to the Lord your God in the desert. Only you must not go very far. Do pray for me.

Moses   I am going to go out from you and pray to the Lord, and the swarms of flies will go away from Pharaoh, from his servants, and from his people tomorrow. Only do not let Pharaoh deal falsely again by not releasing the people to sacrifice to the Lord.

Narrator   So Moses went out from Pharaoh and prayed to the Lord, and the Lord did as Moses asked-he removed the swarms of flies, from Pharaoh, from his servants, and from his people. Not one remained! But Pharaoh hardened his hear this time also and did not release the people. Then the Lord said to Moses...

Lord   Go to Pharaoh and tell him, Thus says the Lord, the God of the Hebrews, Release my people that they may serve me! For if you refuse to release them and continue holding them, then the hand of the Lord will surely bring a very terrible plague on your livestock in the field, on the horses, the donkeys, the camels, the herds, and the flocks. But the Lord will distinguish between the livestock of Israel and the livestock of Egypt, and nothing will die of all that the Israelites have.

Narrator   Then the Lord set an appointed time...

Lord   Tomorrow the Lord will do this thing in the land.

Narrator   And the Lord did this on the next day; all the livestock of the Egyptians died, but of the Israelites livestock not one died. Pharaoh sent representatives to investigate and indeed, not even one of the livestock of Israel had died. But Pharaoh's heart remained hard, and he did not release the people. Then the Lord said to Moses and Aaron....

Lord   Take handfuls of soot from a furnace, and have Moses throw it unto the air while Pharaoh is watching. It will become fine dust over the whole land of Egypt and will cause boils to break out and fester on both people and animals in all the land of Egypt.

Narrator   So they took soot from a furnace and stood before Pharaoh. Moses threw it into the sir, and it caused festering boils to break out on both people and animals. The magicians could not stand before Moses because of the boils, for boils were on the magicians and on all the Egyptians. But the Lord hardened Pharaoh's heart, and he did not listen to them, just as the Lord had predicted to Moses. The Lord said to Moses...

Lord   Get up early in the morning stand before Pharaoh, and tell him, Thus says the Lord, the God of the Hebrews: Release my people so that they may serve me! For this time I will send all my plagues on your very self and on your servants and your people, so that you may know that there is no one like me in all the earth. For by now I could have stretched out my hand and struck you and your people with plague, and you would have been destroyed from the earth. But for this purpose I have caused you to stand; to show you my strength, and so that my name may be declared in all the earth. You are still exalting yourself against my people by not releasing them. I am going to cause very severe hail to rain down about this time tomorrow, such hail as has never occurred in Egypt from the day it was founded until now. So now, send instructions to gather your livestock and all your possessions in the field to a safe place. Every person or animal caught in the field and not brought into the house-the hail will come down on them, and they will die!

Narrator   Those of Pharaoh's servants who feared the word of the Lord hurried to bring their servants and livestock into the houses, but those who did not take the word of the Lord seriously left their servants and their cattle in the field. Then the Lord said to Moses.

Lord   Extend your hand toward the sky that there may be hail in all the land of Egypt, on people and on animals, and on everything that grows in the field in the land of Egypt.

Narrator   When Moses extended his staff toward the sky, the Lord sent thunder and hail, and fire fell on the earth, so the Lord caused hail to rain down on the land of Egypt. Hail fell and fire mingled with the hail; the hail was so severe that there had not been any like it in all the land of Egypt since it had become a nation. The hail struck everything in the open fields, both people and animals, throughout all the land of Egypt. The hail struck everything that grows in the field, and it broke all the trees of the field to pieces. Only in the land of Goshen, where the Israelites lived, was there no hail. So Pharaoh sent and summoned Moses and Aaron and said to them.

Pharaoh   I have sinned this time! The Lord is righteous, and I and my people are guilty. Pray to the Lord, for the mighty thunderings and hail are too much! I will release you and your will stay no longer.

Moses   When I leave the city I will spread my hands to the Lord, the thunder will cease, and there will be no more hail, so that you may know that the earth belongs to the Lord. But as for you and your servants, I know that you do not yet fear the Lord God.

Narrator   (Now the flax and the barley were struck by the hail, for the barley had ripened and the flax was in bud. But the wheat and the spelt were not struck, for they are later crops.) So Moses left Pharaoh, went out of the city, and spread out his hands to the Lord, and the thunder and the hail ceased, and the rain stopped pouring on the earth. When Pharaoh saw that the rain and hail and thunder ceased, he sinned again; both he and his servants hardened their hearts. So Pharaoh's hear remained hard. And he did not release the Israelites, as the Lord had predicted through Moses. The Lord said to Moses.

Lord   Go to Pharaoh, for I have hardened his heart and the heart of his servants, in order to display these signs of mine before him, and in order that in the hearing of your son and your grandson you may tell how I made fools of the Egyptians and about my signs that I displayed among them, so that you may know that I am the Lord.

Narrator   So Moses and Aaron came in to Pharaoh and told him...

Moses   Thus says the Lord, the God of the Hebrews; How long do you refuse to humble yourself before me? Release my people so that they may serve me! But if you refuse to release my people, I am going to bring locust into your territory tomorrow. They will cover the surface of the earth, so that you will be unable to see the ground. They will eat the remainder of what escaped-what is left over for you-from the hail, and they will eat every tree that grows for you from the field. They will fill you houses, the houses of the servants, and all the houses of Egypt, such as neither your fathers nor your grandfathers have seen since they have been in the land until this day!

Narrator   Then Moses turned and went out from Pharaoh. Pharaoh's servants said to him..

Servants   How long will this man be menace to us? Release the people so that they may serve the Lord their God. Do you not know that Egypt is destroyed?

Narrator   So Moses and Aaron were brought back to Pharaoh, and he said to them...

Pharaoh   Go, serve the Lord your God. Exactly who is going with you?

Moses   We will go with our young and our old, with our sons and our daughters, and with our sheep and our cattle we will go, because we are to hold a pilgrim feast for the Lord.

Pharaoh   The Lord will need to be with you if I release you and your dependents! Watch out! Trouble is right in front of you! No! Go, you men only, and serve the Lord, for that is what you want.

Narrator   Then Moses and Aaron were driven out of Pharaoh's presence. The Lord said to Moses...

Lord   Extend your hand over the land of Egypt for the locusts, that they may come up over the land of Egypt and eat everything that grows in the ground, everything that the hail as left.

Narrator   So Moses extended his staff over the land of Egypt, and then the Lord brought an east wind on the land all that day and all night The morning came, and the east wind had brought up the locusts! The locusts went up over all the land of Egypt and settled down in all the territory of Egypt. It was very severe; there had been no locusts like them before, nor will there be such ever again. They covered the surface of all the ground, so that the ground became dark with them, and they ate all the vegetation of the ground and all the fruit of the trees that the hail had left. Nothing green remained on the trees or on anything that grew in the fields throughout the whole land of Egypt. Then Pharaoh quickly summoned Moses and Aaron and said...

Pharaoh   I have sinned against the Lord your God and against you! So now, forgive my sin this time only and pray to the Lord you God that he would only take this death away from me.

Narrator   Moses went out from Pharaoh and prayed to the Lord,and the Lord turned a very strong west wind, and it picked up the locust and blew them into the Red Sea. Not one locust remained in all the territory of Egypt. But the Lord hardened Pharaoh's heart, and he did not release the Israelites.

Lord   Extend your hand toward heaven so that there may be darkness over the land of Egypt, a darkness to thick it can be felt.

Narrator   So Moses extended his hand toward heaven, and there was absolute darkness throughout the land of Egypt for three days. No one could see another person, and no one could rise from his place for three days. But the Israelites had light in the places where they lived. Then Pharaoh summoned Moses and said...

Pharaoh   Go, serve the Lord-only your flocks and herds will be detained. Even your families may go with you.

Moses   Will you also provide us with sacrifices and burnt offerings that we may present them to the Lord our God? Our livestock, must also go with us! Not a hoof is to be left behind! For we must take these animals to serve the Lord our God. Until we arrive there, we do not know what we must use to serve the Lord.

Narrator   But the Lord hardened Pharaoh's heart, and he was not willing to release them.

Pharaoh   Go from me! Watch out for yourself! Do not appear before me again, for when you see my face you will die!

Moses   As you wish! I will not see your face again.

The Passover

Exodus 11: 1 – 12:36 (NET)

You will need:

Actors
- Narrator
- Lord
- Moses
- Pharaoh
- Egyptians (one speaking)
- Israelites (non-speaking)

Props
- Gold
- Silver
- Lamb
- Blood
- Unleavened bread
- Hyssop
- Staff

Tips:

- Cover the door frame with card stock so the students can apply the blood.
- Use fake blood from a costume shop.
- A hyssop is a plant; use a branch or leaf to apply the blood.

Set the scene:

The Israelites were captives of Pharaoh in Egypt and were not able to worship God. They wanted to leave, but Pharaoh did not want them to go because they were the workforce in Egypt. God sent plagues to their land. They were plagued with blood, frogs, lice, flies, livestock, boils, hail, locust and darkness. Pharaoh still refused to let the Israelites go.

Discussion ideas:

- Jews celebrate the Passover today to give thanks to God for saving them from death and bringing them out of slavery. Believers today have experienced salvation as well. We were delivered from spiritual death and slavery to sin.

Christians celebrate the Lord's Supper to reflect on their deliverance from sin and give thanks for new life.

- Do you ever struggle with sin? Remember that God has delivered you by sending His son to die on the cross. Focus on His promise of new life with Him.

Narrator   And the Lord said to Moses...

Lord   I will bring one more plague on Pharaoh and on Egypt; after that he will release you from this place. When he releases you, he will drive you out completely from this place. Instruct the people that each man and each woman is to request from his or her neighbor items of silver and gold.

Narrator   (Now the Lord granted the people favor with the Egyptians. Moreover, the man Moses was very great in the land of Egypt, respected by Pharaoh's servants and by the Egyptian people.)

Moses   Thus says the Lord; About midnight I will go throughout Egypt, and all the firstborn in the land of Egypt will die, from the firstborn son of Pharaoh who sits on his throne, to the firstborn son of the slave girl who is at her hand mill, and all the firstborn of the cattle. There will be a great cry throughout the whole land of Egypt, such as there has never been, nor ever will be again. But against any of the Israelites not even a dog will bark against either people or animals, so that you may know that the Lord distinguishes between Egypt and Israel. All these your servants will come down to me and bow down to me, saying, Go, you and all the people who follow you, and after that I will go out.

Narrator   Then Moses went out from Pharaoh in great anger.

Lord   Pharaoh will not listen to you, so that my wonders may be multiplied in the land of Egypt.

Narrator   So Moses and Aaron did all these wonders before Pharaoh, but the Lord hardened Pharaoh's heart, and he did not release the Israelites from his land. The Lord said to Moses and Aaron in the land of Egypt.

Lord   This month is to be your beginning of months; it will be your first month of the year. Tell the whole community of Israel, In the tenth day of this month they each must take a lamb for themselves according to their families-a lamb for each household. If any household is too small for a lamb, the man and his next door neighbor are to take a lamb according to the number of people-you will make your count for the lamb according to how much each one can eat. Your lamb must be perfect, a male, one year old, you may take it from the sheep or from the goats. You must care for it until the fourteenth day of this month, and then the whole community of Israel will kill it around sundown. They will take some of the blood and put it on the two side posts and top of the doorframe of the houses where they will eat it. They will eat the meat the same night, they will eat it roasted over the fire with bread made without yeast and with bitter herbs. Do not eat it raw or boiled in water, but roast it over the fire with its head, it legs, and its entrails. You must leave nothing until morning, but you must burn with fire whatever remains of it until morning. This is how you are to eat it-dressed to travel, your sandals on your feet, and your staff in your hand. You are to eat it in haste. It is the Lord's Passover. I will pass through the land of Egypt in the same night, and I will attack all the firstborn in the land of Egypt, both of humans and of animals, and on all the gods of Egypt I will execute judgment. I am the Lord. The blood will be a sign for you on the houses where you are, so that when I see the blood I will pass over you, and this plague will not fall on you to destroy you when I attack the land of Egypt. This day will become a memorial for you, and you will celebrate it as a festival to the Lord-you will celebrate it perpetually as a lasting ordinance. For seven days you must eat bread made without yeast. Surely on the first day you must put away yeast from your houses because anyone who eats bread made with yeast from the first day to the seventh day will be cut off from Israel. On the first day there will be a holy convocation, and on the seventh day there will be a holy convocation for you. You must do no work of any kind on them, only what every person will eat-that alone may be prepared for you. So you will keep the Feast of Unleavened Bread, because on this very day I brought your regiments out from the land of Egypt, and so you must keep this day perpetually as a lasting ordinance. In the first month, from the fourteenth day of the month, in the evening you will eat bread made without yeast until the twenty-first day of the month in the evening. For seven days yeast must not be found in your houses, for whoever eats what is made with yeast-that person will be cut off from the community of Israel, whether a foreigner or one born in the land. You will not eat anything made with yeast; in all the places where you live you must eat bread made without yeast.

Narrator   Then Moses summoned all the elders of Israel, and told them.

Moses   Go and select for yourselves a lamb or young goat for your families, and kill the Passover animals. Take a branch of hyssop, dip it in the blood that is in the basin and apply to the top of the doorframe and the two side posts some of the blood that is in the basin. Not one of you is to go out the door of his house until morning. For the Lord will pass through to strike Egypt, and when he sees the blood on the top of the doorframe and the two side posts, then the Lord will pass over the door, and he will not permit the destroyer to enter your houses to strike you. You must observe this event as an ordinance for you and for your children forever. When you enter the land that the Lord will give to you, just as he said, you must observe this ceremony. When your children ask you, 'What does this ceremony mean to you?' then you will say, It is the sacrifice of the Lord's Passover, when He passed over the houses of the Israelites in Egypt, when he struck Egypt and delivered our households.

Narrator   The people bowed down low to the ground, and the Israelites went away and did exactly as the Lord had commanded Moses and Aaron. It happened at midnight-the Lord attacked all the firstborn in the land of Egypt, from the firstborn of Pharaoh who sat on his throne to the firstborn of the captive who was in the prison, and all the firstborn of the cattle. Pharaoh got up in the night, along with all his servants and all Egypt, and there was a great cry in Egypt, for there was no house in which there was not someone dead. Pharaoh summoned Moses and Aaron in the night and said...

Pharaoh   Get up, get out from among my people, both you and the Israelites! Go, serve the Lord as you have requested! Also, take your flocks and your herds just as you have requested! Also, take your flock and your herds, just as you have requested, and leave. But bless me also.

Narrator   The Egyptians were urging the people on, in order to send them out of the land quickly, for they were saying.

Egyptian   We are all dead!

Narrator   So the people took their dough before the yeast was added, with their kneading troughs bound up in their clothing on their shoulders. Now the Israelites had done as Moses told them-they had requested from the Egyptians silver and gold items and clothing. The Lord gave the people favor in the sight of the Egyptians, and they gave them whatever they wanted, and so they plundered Egypt.

Crossing the Red Sea

Exodus 13: 17 – 14:31 (NET)

You will need:

Actors

      Narrator

      Lord

      Moses

      Israelites (one speaking)

      Egyptians (one speaking)

      Angel (non-speaking)

Props

      Bones of Joseph

      Rod / Staff

      Sea

      Chariot

Tips:

- Designate areas for Succoth, Etham, Pi Hahiroth, Migdol, Baal Zephon, and the Red Sea.
- Use a brown sheet over chairs to make a chariot.
- Use a sheet over chairs for the river, and drop or separate the sheet to make the river dry.
- Use a small skeleton from a party store and put it in a jewelry box for the bones.

Set the scene:

The Israelites were captives of Pharaoh in Egypt and were not able to worship God. They wanted to leave, but Pharaoh did not want them to go because they were the workforce in Egypt. God sent plagues to their land. They were plagued with blood, frogs, lice, flies, livestock, boils, hail, locust and darkness. With the last plague, the death of the firstborn, Pharaoh urged the Israelites to leave quickly.

Discussion ideas:

- The Israelites felt doomed as they approached the Red Sea. Their response was fear and despair even though God had provided for them many times. Why do you think they didn't trust God?
- In what ways has God provided for you and proven himself to be faithful?
- Have you ever felt doomed, like the Israelites, over your circumstances? We should trust God to provide for us because he has already proven to be faithful. Is that easy? Why, or why not.

Narrator	When Pharaoh released the people, God did not lead them by the way to the land of the Philistines, although that was nearby, for God said...
God	Lest the people change their minds and return to Egypt when they experience war.
Narrator	So God brought the people around by the way of the desert to the Red Sea, and the Israelites went up from the land of Egypt prepared for battle. Moses took the bones of Joseph with him, for Joseph had made the Israelites solemnly swear, "God will surely attend to you, and you will carry my bones up from this place with you." They journeyed from Sukkoth and camped in Etham, on the edge of the desert. Now the Lord was going before them by day in a pillow of cloud to lead them in the way and by night in a pillar of fire to give them light, so that they could travel day or night. He did not remove the pillar of cloud by day nor the pillar of fire by night from before the people. The Lord spoke to Moses...
Lord	Tell the Israelites, that they must turn and camp before Pi-hahiroth, between Migdol and the sea; you are to camp by the sea before Baal Zephon opposite it. Pharaoh will think regarding the Israelites, 'They are wandering around confused in the land-the desert has closed in on them. I will harden Pharaoh's heart, and he will chase after them. I will gain honor because of Pharaoh and because of all his army, and the Egyptians will know that I am the Lord.
Narrator	So this is what they did. When it was reported to the king of Egypt that the people had fled, the heart of Pharaoh and his servants was turned against the people, and the king and his servants said...
Pharaoh	What in the world have we done? For we have released the people of Israel from serving us!
Narrator	Then he prepared his chariots and took his army with him. He took six hundred select chariots, and all the rest of the chariots of Egypt, and officers on all of them. But the Lord hardened the heart of Pharaoh king of Egypt, and he chased after the Israelites. Now the Israelites were going out defiantly. The Egyptians chased after them, and all the horses and chariots of Pharaoh and his horsemen and his army overtook them camping by the sea, beside Pi-hahiroth, before Baal

Zephon. When Pharaoh got closer, the Israelites looked up, and there were the Egyptians marching after them, and they were terrified. The Israelites cried out to the Lord and they said to Moses.

Israelite   Is it because there are no graves in Egypt that you have taken us away to die in the desert? What in the world have you done to us by bringing us out of Egypt? Isn't this what we told you in Egypt, Leave us alone so that we can serve the Egyptians, because it is better for us to serve the Egyptians than to die in the desert!

Moses   Do not fear! Stand firm and see the salvation of the Lord that He will provide for you today; for the Egyptians that you see today you will never, ever see again. The Lord will fight for you, and you can be still.

Narrator   And the Lord said to Moses...

Lord   Why do you cry out to me? Tell the Israelites to move on. And as for you, lift up your staff and extend your hand toward the sea and divide it, so that the Israelites may go through the middle of the sea on dry ground. And as for me, I am going to harden the hearts of the Egyptians so that they will come after them, that I may be honored because of Pharaoh and his army and his chariots and his horsemen. And the Egyptians will know that I am the Lord when I have gained my honor because of Pharaoh, his chariots, and his horsemen.

Narrator   The angel of God, who was going before the camp of Israel, moved and went behind them, and the pillar of cloud moved from before them and stood behind them. It came between the Egyptian camp and the Israelite camp, it was a dark cloud and it lit up the night so that one camp did not come near the other the whole night. Moses stretched out his hand toward the sea, and the Lord drove the sea apart by a strong east wind all that night, and he made the sea into dry land, and the water was divided. So the Israelites went through the middle of the sea on dry ground, the water forming a wall for them on their right and on the left. The Egyptians chased them and followed them into the middle of the sea-all the horses of Pharaoh, his chariots, and his horsemen. In the morning watch the Lord looked down on the Egyptian army through the pillar of fire and cloud, and he threw the Egyptian army into a panic. He jammed the wheels of their chariots so that they had difficulty driving, and the Egyptians said.

Egyptian   Let's flee from Israel, for the Lord fights for them against Egypt!

Lord   [to Moses] Extend your hand toward the sea, so that the waters my flow back on the Egyptians, on their chariots, and on their housemen!

Narrator   So Moses extended his hand toward the sea, and the sea returned to its normal state when the sun began to rise. Now the Egyptians were fleeing before it, but the Lord overthrew the Egyptians in the middle of the sea. The water returned and covered the chariots and the horsemen and all the army of Pharaoh that was coming after the Israelites into the sea-not so much as one of them survived! But the Israelites walked on dry ground in the middle of the sea; the water forming a wall for them on their right and on their left. So the Lord saved Israel on that day from the power of the Egyptians, and Israel saw the Egyptians dead on the shore of the sea. When Israel saw the great power that the Lord had exercised over the Egyptians, they feared the Lord, and they believed in the Lord and in his servant Moses.

Manna and Quail

Exodus 16: 1-26 (ESV)

You will need:

Actors   Props

    Narrator   Quail

    Israelites (one speaking)   Manna

    Lord

    Moses

    Aaron (non-speaking)

Tips:

- Designate areas for Elim, Sin, and Sinai.
- Use individually wrapped candy for manna so it can be picked up from the floor.
- Use a different kind of candy for quail, or use stuffed animals that actors can pretend to cook and eat.

Set the scene:

The Israelites have been delivered from the Egyptians. God brought them across the Red Sea and into the wilderness. There were about 600,000 of them.

Discussion ideas:

- The Israelites were faced with a difficult situation and it led to stress and complaining. They wanted to go back to Egypt. Do you think they liked being in Egypt? No, they were just looking for an escape from their situation. When pressure comes your way, don't focus on the quick escape. Instead ask God to help you deal with the cause of your stress.
- Has God helped you through a difficult time?
- Why do you think God told the Israelites not to work on the Sabbath? It is easy to let our busy lifestyles and responsibilities take over our schedules and not leave time to worship. Do you intentionally make time for God?

Narrator   They set out from Elim, and all the congregation of the people of Israel came to the wilderness of Sin, which is between Elim, and Sinai, on the fifteenth day of the second month after they had departed from the land of Egypt. And the whole congregation of the people of Israel grumbled against Moses and Aaron in the wilderness, and the people of Israel said to them...

Israelites   Would that we had died by the hand of the Lord in the land of Egypt, when we sat by the meat pots and ate bread to the full, for you have brought us out into this wilderness to kill this whole assembly with hunger.

Narrator   Then the Lord said to Moses...

Lord   Behold, I am about to rain bread from heaven for you, and the people shall go out and gather a day's portion every day, that I may test them, whether they will walk in my law or not. On the sixth day, when they prepare what they bring in, it will be twice as much as they gather daily.

Narrator   So Moses and Aaron said to all the people of Israel...

Moses   At evening you shall know that it was the Lord who brought you out of the land of Egypt, and in the morning you shall see the glory of the Lord, because he has heard your grumbling against the Lord. For what are we, that you grumble against us? When the Lord gives you in the evening meat to eat and in the morning bread to the full, because the Lord has heard your grumbling that you grumble against him—what are we? Your grumbling is not against us but against the Lord.

Narrator   Then Moses said to Aaron...

Moses   Say to the whole congregation of the people of Israel, 'Come near before the Lord, for he has heard your grumbling.'

Narrator   And as soon as Aaron spoke to the whole congregation of the people of Israel, they looked toward the wilderness, and behold, the glory of the Lord appeared in the cloud. And the Lord said to Moses...

Lord   I have heard the grumbling of the people of Israel. Say to them, 'At twilight you shall eat meat and in the morning you shall be filled with bread. Then you shall know that I am the Lord your God.

Narrator   In the evening quail came up and covered the camp, and in the morning dew lay around the camp. And when the dew had gone up, there was on the face of the wilderness a fine, flake-like thing, fine as frost on the ground. When the people of Israel saw it, they said to one another...

Israelites What is it?

Narrator   For they did not know what it was. And Moses said to them...

Moses   It is bread that the Lord has given you to eat. This is what the Lord has commanded: Gather of it, each one of you, as much as he can eat. You shall each take an omer, according to the number of the persons that each of you has in his tent.

Narrator   And the people of Israel did so. They gathered, some more, some less. But when they measured it with an omer, whoever gathered much had nothing left over, and whoever gathered little had no lack. Each of them gathered as much as he could eat. And Moses said to them...

Moses   Let no one leave any of it over till the morning.

Narrator   But they did not listen to Moses. Some left part of it till the morning, and it bred worms and stank. And Moses was angry with them. Morning by morning they gathered it, each as much as he could eat; but when the sun grew hot, it melted. On the sixth day they gathered twice as much bread, two omers each. And when all the leaders of the congregation came and told Moses, he said to them...

Moses   This is what the Lord has commanded: 'Tomorrow is a day of solemn rest, a holy Sabbath to the Lord; bake what you will bake and boil what you will boil, and all that is left over lay aside to be kept till the morning.

Narrator   So they laid it aside till the morning, as Moses commanded them and it did not stink, and there were no worms in it. Moses said...

Moses   Eat it today, for today is a Sabbath to the Lord; today you will not find it in the field. Six days you shall gather it, but on the seventh day, which is a Sabbath, there will be none.

Water From the Rock

Exodus 17: 1-7 (ESV)

You will need:

Actors   Props

    Narrator   Rock

    Israelites (one speaking)   Staff

    Moses   Water bottles

    Lord

    Elders (non-speaking)

Tips:

- Designate areas for Sin and Rephidim.
- Create a rock from a large brown paper bag, slightly crumbled, and place small water bottles under the bag. If possible, include enough water bottles for everyone in the class.

Set the scene:

Moses had taken the people out of Egypt and God had provided them with food (manna) to sustain them. But, they were traveling through the wilderness and had no water.

Discussion ideas:

- Have you had a need that you were sure would never be met? What did you do? The Israelites complained about their problem. Does complaining help? No, it just causes more stress and leads to more complaining. When we have a need, we should turn to God. He can help us think clearly to find a solution to our problem and also give us comfort during the time that we must wait for our need to be met.

- The Israelites were so thirsty and there was no water in sight. Again, God provided for their needs in an unexpected way. We should remember to turn to God and seek his provision for our needs, even when it seems impossible. Our God can do the impossible.

Narrator	All the congregation of the people of Israel moved on from the wilderness of Sin by stages, according to the commandment of the Lord, and camped at Rephidim, but there was no water for the people to drink. Therefore the people quarreled with Moses and said...
Israelites	Give us water to drink.
Moses	Why do you quarrel with me? Why do you test the Lord?
Narrator	But the people thirsted there for water, and the people grumbled against Moses and said...
Israelites	Why did you bring us up out of Egypt, to kill us and our children and our livestock with thirst?
Narrator	So Moses cried to the Lord...
Moses	What shall I do with this people? They are almost ready to stone me.
Lord	Pass on before the people, taking with you some of the elders of Israel, and take in your hand the staff with which you struck the Nile, and go. Behold, I will stand before you there on the rock of Horeb, and you shall strike the rock, and water shall come out of it, and the people will drink.
Narrator	And Moses did so, in the sight of the elders of Israel. And he called the name of the place Massah and Meribah, because of the quarreling of the people of Israel, and because they tested the Lord by saying, "Is the Lord among us or not?

The Golden Calf

Exodus 32: 1-26 (ESV)

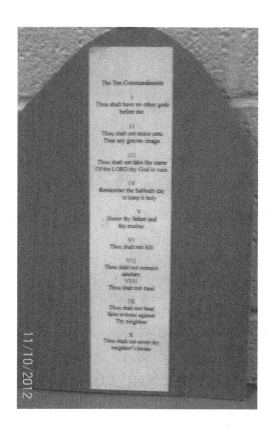

You will need:

Actors	Props
Narrator	Gold jewelry/ear rings
Aaron	Golden calf
Lord	Altar
Joshua	Tablet of Ten Commandments
Israelites (one speaking)	Sticks for fire

Tips:

- Designate and area for the wilderness and an area for Mount Sinai.
- Use a stuffed animal for the golden calf or paint a plastic toy animal.
- Use card stock, or cardboard, to make a tablet for the Ten Commandments.

- Use a flashlight with sticks to create a fire, or cut flames from red and orange paper.

Set the scene:

Moses is still leading the Israelites through the wilderness. Remember, God had rescued them from the Egyptians, brought them across the red sea, and provided food and water for them. Moses went up on Mount Sinai to be with God. He was gone for nearly six weeks and the people were panicking.

Discussion ideas:

- The Israelites panicked when Moses didn't come back as quickly as they thought he should. Instead of remembering how God had been faithful to them in the past, they wanted an idol to worship. Worshipping a golden calf might seem silly to us, but many people worship "things" instead of God. We need to remember to rely on God and keep our focus on Him when we are in tough situations or start to feel panicked over something. God is faithful and has a plan for us.
- The Israelites created the golden calf so they could have something physical to worship. Did they break any of God's commandments? Which one?
- Did God know they were worshipping an idol? Yes, God told Moses that the people were sinning and that He wanted to destroy them. Moses pleaded with God not to destroy them. Because of this God relented, which means to soften or become more compassionate.

Narrator	When the people saw that Moses delayed to come down from the mountain, the people gathered themselves together to Aaron and said to him...
Israelites	Up, make us gods who shall go before us. As for this Moses, the man who brought us up out of the land if Egypt, we do not know what has become of him.
Aaron	Take off the rings of gold that are in the ears of your wives, your sons, and your daughters, and bring them to me.
Narrator	So all the people took off the rings of gold that were in their ears and brought them to Aaron. And he received the gold from their hand and fashioned it with a graving tool and made a golden calf. And they said...
Israelites	These are your gods, O Israel, who brought you up out of the land of Egypt! When Aaron saw this, he built an altar before it. And Aaron made a proclamation and said...
Aaron	Tomorrow shall be a feast to the Lord.
Narrator	And they rose up early the next day and offered burnt offerings and brought peace offerings. And the people sat down to eat and drink and rose up to play.
Lord	[to Moses] Go down, for your people, whom you brought up out of the land of Egypt, have corrupted themselves. They have turned aside quickly out of the way that I commanded them. They have made for themselves a golden calf and have worshiped it and sacrificed to it and said, 'These are your gods, O Israel, who brought you up out of the land of Egypt! I have seen this people, and behold, it is a stiff-necked people. Now therefore let me alone, that my wrath may burn hot against them and I may consume them, in order that I may make a great nation of you.
Moses	O Lord, why does your wrath burn hot against your people, whom you have brought out of the land of Egypt with great power and with a mighty hand? Why should the Egyptians say, 'With evil intent did he bring them out, to kill them in the mountains and to consume them from the face of the earth?' Turn from your burning anger and relent from this disaster against your people.

Remember Abraham, Isaac, and Israel, you servants, to whom you swore by your own self, and said to them, 'I will multiply your offspring as the stars of heaven, and all this land that I have promised I will give to your offspring, and they shall inherit it forever.'

Narrator   And the Lord relented from the disaster that he had spoken of bringing on his people. Then Moses turned and went down from the mountain with the two tablets of the testimony in his hand, tablets that were written on both sides; on the front and on the back they were written. The tablets were the work of God, and the writing was the writing of God, engraved on the tablets. When Joshua heard the noise of the people as they shouted, he said to Moses...

Joshua   There is a noise of war in the camp. It is not the sound of shouting for victory, or the sound of cry of defeat, but the sound of singing that I hear. And as soon as he came near the camp and saw the calf and the dancing, Moses' anger burned hot, and he threw the tablets out of his hands and broke them at the foot of the mountain. He took the calf that they had made and burned it with fire and ground it to powder and scattered it on the water and made the people of Israel drink it. And Moses said to Aaron...

Moses   What did the people do to you that you have brought such a great sin upon them?

Aaron   Let not the anger of my lord burn hot. You know the people, that they are set on evil. For they said to me, 'Make us gods who shall go before us. As for this Moses, the man who brought us up out of the land of Egypt, we do not know what has become of him.' So I said to them, 'let any who have gold take it off.' So they gave it to me, and I threw it into the fire, and out came this calf.

Narrator   And when Moses saw that the people had broken loose (for Aaron had let them break loose to the derision of their enemies), then Moses stood in the gate of the camp and said...

Moses   Who is on the Lord's side? Come to me.

Narrator   And all the sons of Levi gathered around him.

Moses Explores Canaan

Numbers 13: 1 – 14:24 (NLT)

You will need:

Actors   Props

    Narrator   Grapes

    Lord   Pomegranates

    Moses   Figs (if available)

    Caleb   Pole for grapes

    Israelites (one speaking)

    Tribe (one speaking)

    Aaron (non-speaking)

    Joshua (non-speaking)

Tips:

- Designate an area for the Wilderness of Paran and an area for the Valley of Eschol.
- If real fruit is unavailable, use toy fruit or pictures.
- Remind the students that each of these tribes came from the sons of Jacob.

Set the scene:

Moses is still leading the Israelites through the wilderness. Remember, God has rescued them form the Egyptians and brought them across the Red Sea and provided food and water for them. It has been nearly 40 years.

Discussion ideas:

- Caleb was a man of courage. He stood boldly before a crowd and voiced an unpopular opinion. As Christians, we will sometime find ourselves in the midst of friends not wanting to follow God's plan. Have you been in a similar situation? How did you handle it? What happened

- Once again, the Israelites lost hope and wanted to return to Egypt. Once again, the Lord said he wanted to destroy them. Once again, Moses interceded for them and asked for forgiveness for the sins of the Israelites, and the Lord agrees to forgive them. We can learn from the mistakes of the Israelites. When we are in difficult situations, we can trust God to be faithful. The Lord blessed Caleb for trusting him and remaining faithful even when those around him weren't. It is good to know that God will bless our obedience too.

Narrator   The Lord now said to Moses...

Lord   Send out men to explore the land of Canaan, the land I am giving to the Israelites. Send one leader from each of the twelve ancestral tribes.

Narrator   So Moses did as the Lord commanded him. He sent out twelve men, all tribal leaders of Israel, from their camp in the wilderness of Paran. These were the tribes and the names of their leaders:

Tribe	Leader
Reuben	Shammua son of Zaccur
Simeon	Shaphat son of Hori
Judah	Caleb son of Jephunneh
Issachar	Igal son of Joseph
Ephraim	Hoshea son of Nun
Benjamin	Palti son of Raphu
Zebulun	Gaddiel son of Sodi
Manasseh	Gaddi son of Susi
Dan	Ammiel son of Gemalli
Asher	Sethur son of Michael
Naphtali	Nahbi son of Vophsi
Gad	Geuel son of Maki

These are the names of the men Moses sent out to explore the land. (Moses called Hoshea son of Nun by the name of Joshua.) Moses gave the men these instructions as he sent them out to explore the land...

Moses   Go north through the Negev into the hill country. See what the land is like, and find out whether the people living there are strong or weak, few or many. See what kind of land they live in. Is it good or bad? Do their towns have walls, or are they unprotected like open camps? Is the soil fertile or poor? Are there many trees? Do your best to bring back samples of the crops you see.

Narrator   (It happened to be the season for harvesting the first ripe grapes.) So they went up and explored the land from the wilderness of Zin as far as Rehob, near Lebohamath. Going north, they passed through the Negev and arrived at

Hebron, where Ahiman, Sheshai, and Talmai—all descendants of Anak—lived. (The ancient town of Hebron was founded seven years before the Egyptian city of Zoan.) When they came to the valley of Eshcol, they cut down a branch with a single cluster of grapes so large that it took two of them to carry it on a pole between them! They also brought back samples of the pomegranates and figs. That place was called the valley of Eshcol (which means "cluster"), because of the cluster of grapes the Israelite men cut there. After exploring the land for forty days, the men returned to Moses, Aaron, and the whole community of Israel at Kadesh in the wilderness of Paran. They reported to the whole community what they had seen and showed them the fruit they had taken from the land. This was their report to Moses...

Tribe   We entered the land you sent us to explore, and it is indeed a bountiful country—a land flowing with milk and honey. Here is the kind of fruit it produces. But the people living there are powerful, and their towns are large and fortified. We even saw giants there, the descendants of Anak! The Amalekites live in the Negev, and Hittites, Jebusites, and Amorites live in the hill country. The Canaanites live along the coast of the Mediterranean Sea and along the Jordan valley.

Narrator   But Caleb tried to quiet the people as they stood before Moses.

Caleb   Let's go at once to take the land. We can certainly conquer it!

Narrator   But the other men who had explored the land with him disagreed.

Tribe   We can't go up against them! They are stronger than we are!

Narrator   So they spread this bad report about the land among the Israelites...

Tribe   The land we traveled through and explored will devour anyone who goes to live there. All the people we saw were huge. We even saw giants there, the descendants of Anak. Next to them we felt like grasshoppers, and that's what they thought, too!

Narrator	Then the whole community began weeping aloud, and they cried all night. Their voices rose in a great chorus of protest against Moses and Aaron.
Israelites	If only we had died in Egypt, or even here in the wilderness! Why is the Lord taking us to this country only to have us die in battle? Our wives and our little ones will be carried off as plunder! Wouldn't it be better for us to return to Egypt?
Narrator	Then they plotted among themselves.
Israelites	Let's choose a new leader and go back to Egypt!
Narrator	Then Moses and Aaron fell face down on the ground before the whole community of Israel. Two of the men who had explored the land, Joshua son of Nun and Caleb son of Jephunneh, tore their clothing. They said to all the people of Israel...
Caleb	The land we traveled through and explored is a wonderful land! And if the Lord is pleased with us, he will bring us safely into that land and give it to us. It is a rich land flowing with milk and honey. Do not rebel against the Lord, and don't be afraid of the people of the land. They are only helpless prey to us! They have no protection, but the Lord is with us! Don't be afraid of them!
Narrator	But the whole community began to talk about stoning Joshua and Caleb. Then the glorious presence of the Lord appeared to all the Israelites at the Tabernacle. And the Lord said to Moses...
Lord	How long will these people treat me with contempt? Will they never believe me, even after all the miraculous signs I have done among them? I will disown them and destroy them with a plague. Then I will make you into a nation greater and mightier than they are!
Narrator	But Moses objected.
Moses	What will the Egyptians think when they hear about it? They know full well the power you displayed in rescuing your people from Egypt. Now if you destroy

them, the Egyptians will send a report to the inhabitants of this land, who have already heard that you live among your people. They know, Lord, that you have appeared to your people face to face and that your pillar of cloud hovers over them. They know that you go before them in the pillar of cloud by day and the pillar of fire by night. Now if you slaughter all these people with a single blow, the nations that have heard of your fame will say, 'The Lord was not able to bring them into the land he swore to give them, so he killed them in the wilderness.' Please, Lord, prove that your power is as great as you have claimed. For you said, 'The Lord is slow to anger and filled with unfailing love, forgiving every kind of sin and rebellion. But he does not excuse the guilty. He lays the sins of the parents upon their children; the entire family is affected—even children in the third and fourth generations. In keeping with your magnificent, unfailing love, please pardon the sins of this people, just as you have forgiven them every since they left Egypt.

Lord I will pardon them as you have requested. But as surely as I live, and as surely as the earth is filled with the Lord's glory, not one of these people will ever enter that land. They have all seen my glorious presence and the miraculous signs I performed both in Egypt and in the wilderness, but again and again they have tested me by refusing to listen to my voice. They will never even see the land I swore to give their ancestors. None of those who have treated me with contempt will ever see it. But my servant Caleb has a different attitude than the others have. He has remained loyal to me, so I will bring him into the land he explored. His descendants will possess their full share of that land.

Balaam's Donkey

Numbers 22: 1-38 (NET)

You will need:

Actors   Props

    Narrator   Sword for Angel

    Moab   Staff for Balaam

    Balaam

    Messenger

    God

    Official

    Angel

    Donkey

    Princes (one speaking)

    Balak

Tips:

- Designate areas for Moab, Midian, and Pethor
- For safety, instruct Balaam guide the donkey without riding him.

Set the Scene:

The Israelites are still wondering in the wilderness, but are getting closer to the Promised Land. As you can imagine, the neighboring nations might not want this large crowd of Israelites, about 600,000, in their land.

Discussion ideas:

- Balaam was obeying God in his actions, however he was rebelling in his heart and only thinking about the bribe. Are your thoughts consistent with your actions? When you obey God, are you doing it grudgingly or out of love for Him?
- What about when you obey your parents?

Narrator	The Israelites traveled on and camped in the plains of Moab on the side of the Jordan River across from Jericho. Balak son of Zippor saw all that the Israelites had done to the Amorites. And the Moabites were greatly afraid of the people, because they were so numerous. The Moabites were sick with fear because of the Israelites. So the Moabites said to the elders of Midian...
Moab	Now this mass of people will lick up everything around us, as the bull devours the grass of the field.
Narrator	Now Balak son of Zippor was king of the Moabites at this time. And he sent messengers to Balaam son of Beor at Pethor, which is by the Euphrates River in the land of Amaw, to summon him, saying...
Messenger	Look, a nation has come out of Egypt. They cover the face of the earth, and they are settling next to me. So now please come and curse this nation for me, for they are too powerful for me. Perhaps I will prevail so that we may conquer them, and drive them out of the land. For I know that whoever you bless is blessed, and whoever you curse is cursed.
Narrator	So the elders of Moab and the elders of Midian departed with the fee for divination in their hand. They came to Balaam and reported to him the words of Balak.
Balaam	Stay here tonight, and I will bring back to you whatever word the Lord may speak to me.
Narrator	So the princes of Moab stayed with Balaam. And God came to Balaam and said.
God	Who are these men with you?
Balaam	Balak son of Zippor, king of the Moab, has sent a message to me, saying, "Look, a nation has come out of Egypt, and it covers the face of the earth. Come now and put a curse on them for me; perhaps I will be able to defeat them and drive them out."

God   You must not go with them; you must not curse the people, for they are blessed.

Narrator   So Balaam got up in the morning, and said to the princes of Balak.

Balaam   Go to your land, for the Lord has refused to permit me to go with you.

Narrator   So the princes of Moab departed and went back to Balak and said…

Princes   Balaam refused to come with us.

Narrator   Balak again sent princes, more numerous and more distinguished than the first. And they came to Balaam and said to him…

Princes   Thus says Balak son of Zippor; 'Please do not let anything hinder you from coming to me. For I will honor you greatly, and whatever you tell me I will do. So come, put a curse on this nation for me.

Balaam   Even if Balak would give me his palace full of silver and gold, I could not transgress the commandment of the Lord my God to do less or more. Now therefore, please stay the night here also, that I may know what more the Lord might say to me.

Narrator   God came to Balaam that night, and said to him…

God   If the men have come to call you, get up and go with them, but the word that I will say to you, that you must do.

Narrator   So Balaam got up in the morning, saddled his donkey, and went with the princes of Moab. Then God's anger was kindled because he went, and the angel of the Lord stood in the road to oppose him. Now he was riding on his donkey and his two servants were with him. And the donkey saw the angel of the Lord standing in the road with his sword drawn in his hand, so the donkey turned aside from the road and went into the field. But Balaam beat the donkey, to make her turn back to the road. Then the angel of the Lord stood in a path among the vineyards, where there was a wall on either side. And when the donkey saw the angel of the Lord, she pressed herself into the wall and crushed Balaam's foot against the wall. So he beat her again. Then the angel of the Lord went farther, and stood in a narrow place, where there was no way to turn either to the right or to the left. When the donkey saw the angel of the Lord, she crouched down under Balaam. Then Balaam was angry, and he beat his donkey with a staff. Then the Lord opened the mouth of the donkey, and she said to Balaam.

Donkey   What have I done to you that you have beaten me these three times?

Balaam   You have made me look stupid; I wish there were a sword in my hand, for I would kill you right now.

Donkey   Am not I your donkey that you have ridden ever since I was yours until this day? Have I ever attempted to treat you this way?

Balaam   No.

Narrator   Then the Lord opened Balaam's eyes, and he saw the angel of the Lord standing in the way with his sword drawn in his hand; so he bowed his head and threw himself down with his face to the ground. The angel of the Lord said to him...

Angel   Why have you beaten your donkey these three times? Look, I came out to oppose you because what you are doing is perverse before me. The donkey saw me and turned from me these three times. If she had not turned from me, I would have killed you but saved her alive.

Narrator   Balaam said to the Angel of the Lord...

Balaam   I have sinned, for I did not know that you stood against me in the road. So now, if it is evil in your sight, I will go back home.

Angel   Go with the men, but you may only speak the word that I will speak to you.

Narrator   So Balaam went with the princes of Balak. When Balak heard that Balaam was coming, he went out to meet him at a city of Moab which was on the border of the Amon at the boundary of his territory. Balak said to Balaam.

Balak   Did I not send again and again to you to summon you? Why did you not come to me? Am I not able to honor you?

Balaam   Look, I have come to you. Now, am I able to speak just anything? I must speak only the word that God puts in my mouth.

Joshua Leads the Nation

Joshua 1: 1-11, 2: 1-24 (TLB)

You will need:

Actors

    Narrator

    Lord

    Joshua

    People (one speaks)

    Two spies (one speaks)

    Messenger

    Rahab

Props

    Red Rope

    City wall with Rahab's house

    Area for Rahab's roof

    Stalks of flax

Tips:

- Designate an area for the wilderness with the Israelites and an area for Jericho with Rahab's house at the city wall.
- Use a red belt or ribbon if red rope is not available.
- Place chairs in a rectangle to represent the wall around the city and put a table against one "wall" to be Rahab's house so the spies can leave over the wall of the city. Designate an area to be the roof.
- Use branches as stalks of flax.

Set the Scene:

After 40 years of wandering in the wilderness, the Israelites are finally getting close to entering the Promised Land. Moses has died and Joshua is the new leader.

Discussion ideas:

- Under the circumstances, Rahab had to make a choice and make it quickly. God blessed her despite the lie. Rahab was commended for her faith. God does not expect our judgment to be perfect, but for us to put our trust in Him and do our best. Have you ever faced a dilemma where there didn't seem to be a perfect solution, yet you had to make a decision? What did you do? Was God pleased?

- Rahab had lived a sinful life, but she had heard about what God had done for the Israelites and she decided to trust God and help the spies. God blessed her and saved her whole family because of her faithfulness. Isn't it comforting to know that God can use anyone, even people with a sinful past, if we are willing to trust Him and be faithful and obedient to Him.

Narrator   After the death of Moses, the Lord's disciple, God spoke to Moses' assistant, whose name was Joshua (the son of Nun, and said to him...

Lord   Now that my disciple is dead, (you are the new leader of Israel). Lead my people across the Jordan River into the Promised Land. I say to you what I said to Moses: 'Wherever you go will be part of the land of Israel-all the way from Negeb desert in the south to the Lebanon mountains in the north, and from the Mediterranean Sea in the west to the Euphrates River in the east, including all the land of the Hittites.' No one will be able to oppose you as long as you live, for I will be with you just as I was with Moses; I will not abandon you or fail to help you. Be strong and brave, for you will be a successful leader of my people; and they shall conquer all the land I promised to their ancestors. You need only to be strong and courageous and to obey to the letter every law Moses gave you, for if you are careful to obey every one of them you will be successful in everything you do. Constantly remind the people about these laws, and you yourself must think about them every day and every night so that you will be sure to obey all of them. For only then will you succeed. Yes, be bold and strong! Banish fear and doubt! For remember, the Lord your God is with you wherever you go.

Narrator   Then Joshua issued instructions to the leaders of Israel to tell the people to get ready to cross the Jordan River.

Joshua   In three days we will go across and conquer and live in the land which God has given us!

Narrator   Then Joshua sent two spies from the Israeli camp at Acacia to cross the river and check out the situation on the other side, especially at Jericho. They arrived at an inn operated by a woman named Rahab, who was a prostitute. They were planning to spend the night there, but someone informed the king of Jericho that two Israelis who were suspected of being spies had arrived in the city that evening. He dispatched a police squadron to Rahab's home, demanding that she surrender them. And he explained to her...

Messenger   They are spies. They have been sent by the Israeli leaders to discover the best way to attack us.

Narrator   But she had hidden them, so she told the officer in charge.

Rahab   The men were here earlier, but I didn't know they were spies. They left the city at dusk as the city gates were about to close, and I don't know where they went. If you hurry you can probably catch up with them!

Narrator   But actually she had taken them up to the roof and hidden them beneath piles of flax that were drying there. So the constable and his men went all the way to the Jordan River looking for them; meanwhile, the city gates were kept shut. Rahab went up to talk to the men before they retired for the night.

Rahab   I know perfectly well that your God is going to give my country to you. We are all afraid of you; everyone is terrified if the word Israel is even mentioned . For we have heard how the Lord made a path through the Red Sea for you when you left Egypt! And we know what you did to Sihon and Og, the two Amorite kings east of the Jordan, and how you ruined their land and completely destroyed their people. No wonder we are afraid of you! No one has any fight left in him after hearing things like that, for your God is the supreme God of heaven, not just an ordinary god. Now I beg for this one thing: Swear to me by the sacred name of your God that when Jericho is conquered you will let me live, along with my father and mother, my brothers and sisters, and all their families. This is only fair after the way I have helped you.

Spies   If you won't betray us, we'll see to it that you and your family aren't harmed. We'll defend you with our lives.

Narrator   Then since her house was on top of the city wall, she let them down by a rope from a window.

Rahab   Escape to the mountains. Hide there for three days until the men who are searching for you have returned, then go on your way.

Spies   We cannot be responsible for what happens to you unless this rope is hanging from the window and unless all your relatives-your father, mother, brothers, and anyone else-are here inside the house. If they go out into the street we assume no responsibility whatsoever; but we swear that no one inside this house will be killed or injured. However, if you betray us, then this oath will no longer bind us in any way.

Rahab   I accept your terms.

Narrator   And she left the scarlet rope hanging from the window. The spies went up into the mountains and stayed there three days, until the men who were chasing them had returned to the city after searching everywhere along the road without success. Then the two spies came down from the mountain and crossed the river and reported to Joshua all that had happened to them.

Spies   The Lord will certainly give us the entire land, for all the people over there are scared to death of us.

Crossing the Jordan River

Joshua 3 & 4 (TLB)

You will need:

Actors

    Narrator

    Officers

    Joshua

    Lord

    Priests (non-speaking)

    Israelites (non-speaking)

    12 Men – one from each
       tribe (non-speaking)

Props

    Jordan River

    24 Stones

    Ark of the Covenant

Tips:

- Designate an area for Acacia Grove on one side of the river and areas for Jericho and Gilgal on the other side of the river.
- Use a sheet over chairs for the river and drop the sheet to make the river dry.
- Use a shoe box covered with paper for the Ark of the Covenant and attach a larger piece of cardboard to allow four people to carry it.
- If stones are not available, cover small boxes to make the stones, or use cardboard cutouts.

Set the scene:

After 40 years of wandering in the wilderness, the Israelites are finally getting close to entering the Promised Land. Joshua is their leader and he has already sent spies ahead to gather information.

Discussion idea:

- God showed His great power again to his people as He allowed the Israelites to cross the river. The river was at flood stage, which means close to overflowing, and He not only stopped the water but made the ground dry for them to walk on. Have you ever seen God do something that you thought would be impossible? You may not have witnessed something as bold as this, but God leads us in miraculous ways still today.
- God directed the Israelites to build a memorial after they crossed the Jordan so they could remember this event and share it with the future generations. Have your parents or grandparents shared stores of their faith with you? Do you have a story of your faith?

Narrator	Early the next morning Joshua and all the people of Israel left Acacia, and arrived that evening at the banks of the Jordan River, where they camped for a few days before crossing. On the third day, officers went through the camp giving these instructions :
Officers	When you see the priests carrying the Ark of God, follow them. You have never before been where we are going now, so they will guide you. However, stay about a half mile behind, with a clear space between you and the Ark; be sure that you don't get any closer.
Narrator	Then Joshua told the people to purify themselves.
Joshua	For tomorrow the Lord will do a great miracle.
Narrator	In the morning Joshua ordered the priests.
Joshua	Take up the Ark and lead us across the river!
Narrator	And so they started out.
Lord	[to Joshua] Today, I will give you great honor, so that all Israel will know that I am with you just as I was with Moses. Instruct the priests who are carrying the Ark to stop at the edge of the river.
Narrator	Then Joshua summoned all the people and told them...
Joshua	Come and listen to what the Lord your God has said. Today you are going to know for sure that the living God is among you and that he will, without fail, drive out the Canaanites, Hittites, Hivites, Perizzites, Girgashites, Amorites, and Jebusites-all the people who now live in the land you will soon occupy. Think of it! The Ark of God, who is Lord of the whole earth, will lead you across the river! Now select twelve men, one from each tribe, for a special task. When the priests who are carrying the Ark touch the water with their feet, the river will stop flowing as though held back by a dam, and will pile up as though against an invisible wall!

Narrator	Now it was the harvest season and the Jordan was overflowing all its banks; but as the people set out to cross the river and as the feet of the priests who were carrying the Ark touched the water at the river's edge, suddenly, far up the river at the city of Adam, near Zarethan, the water began piling up as though against a dam! And the water below that point flowed on to the Dead Sea until the riverbed was empty. Then all the people crossed at a spot where the river was as close to the city of Jericho, and the priests who were carrying the Ark stood on dry ground in the middle of the Jordan and waited as all the people passed by. When all the people were safely across, the Lord said to Joshua.
Lord	Tell the twelve men chosen for a special task, one from each tribe, each to take a stone from where the priests are standing in the middle of the Jordan, and to carry them out and pile them up as a monument at the place where you camp tonight.
Narrator	So Joshua summoned the twelve men, and told them...
Joshua	Go out into the middle of the Jordan where the Ark is. Each of you is to carry out a stone on your shoulder-twelve stones in all, one for each of the twelve tribes. We will use them to build a monument so that in the future, when your children ask, "What is this Monument for?' you can tell them, It is to remind us that the Jordan River stopped flowing when the Ark of God went across! The Monument will be a permanent reminder to the people of Israel of this amazing miracle.
Narrator	So the men did as Joshua told them. They took twelve stones from the middle of the Jordan river-one for each tribe, just as the Lord had commanded Joshua. They carried them to the place where they were camped for the night and constructed a monument there. Joshua also built another monument of twelve stones in the middle of the river, at the place where the priests were standing; and it is there to this day. The priests who were carrying the Ark stood in the middle of the river until all these instructions of the Lord, which has been given to Joshua by Moses, had been carried out. Meanwhile, the people had hurried across the riverbed, and when everyone was over, the people watched the priests carry the Ark up out of the riverbed. The troops of Reuben, Gad, and the half-tribe of Manasseh-fully armed as Moses had instructed, and forty thousand

strong-led the other tribes of the Lord's army across to the plains of Jericho. It was a tremendous day for Joshua! The Lord made him great in the eyes of all the people of Israel, and they revered him as much as they had Moses, and respected him deeply all the rest of his life. For it was Joshua who, at the Lord's command, issued the orders to the priests carrying the Ark.

Lord   Come up from the riverbed.

Narrator   The Lord now told him to command them. So Joshua issued the order. And as soon as the priests came out, the water poured down again as usual and overflowed the banks of the river as before! This miracle occurred on the 25th of March. That day the entire nation crossed the Jordan River and camped in Gilgal at the eastern edge of the city of Jericho; and there the twelve stones from the Jordan were piled up as a monument. Then Joshua explained again the purpose of the stones:

Joshua   In the future, when your children ask you why theses stones are here and what they mean, you are to tell them that these stones are a reminder of this amazing miracle-that the nation of Israel crossed the Jordan River on dry ground! Tell them how the Lord our God dried up the river right before our eyes, and then kept it dry until we were all across! It is the same thing the Lord did forty years ago at the Red sea! He did this so that all the nations of the earth will realize that Jehovah is the mighty God, and so that all of you will worship him forever.

The Fall of Jericho

Joshua 5: 13 – 6:27 (TLB)

You will need:

Actors

    Narrator

    Joshua

    Lord

    Commander

    Priests (non-speaking)

    Guard (non-speaking)

    Rahab (non-speaking)

    Armed Men (non-speaking)

    Rahab's Family (non-speaking)

Props

    Ark of the Covenant

    City

    Trumpets

    Red Rope

Tips:

- Use a shoe box covered with paper for the Ark of the Covenant and attach a larger piece of cardboard to allow four people to carry it.
- Place large pieces of cardboard from appliance boxes around chairs in a rectangle to represent the wall around the city and include an area to be Rahab's house.
- Use a red belt or ribbon for the red rope to hang from Rahab's window.
- Use paper towel rolls for the trumpets if you don't have instruments.
- Dim the lights to signify the passing of time between each day.

Set the scene:

The time has come to take over the city that they have been traveling to for 40 years. This is the Promised Land.

Discussion ideas:

- Why did God give all these silly instruction for the battle? Sometime God's instruction to us may require us to do things that don't make sense and it is hard to believe that things will work out. We need to take one day at a time and follow him step by step.

- The walls around Jericho were up to 25 feet tall and 20 feet thick in some places. Do you think the marching and shouting of the Israelites caused the wall to fall? It was a miracle! And the Israelites knew that it was God that caused the walls to fall. The Israelites were obedient and God was faithful.

Narrator   As Joshua was sizing up the city of Jericho, a man appeared nearby with a drawn sword. Joshua strode over to him and demanded.

Joshua   Are you friend or foe?

Commander I am the Commander-in-Chief of the Lord's army.

Narrator   Joshua fell to the ground before him and worshiped him and said...

Joshua   Give me your commands.

Commander Take off your shoes, for this is holy ground.

Narrator   And Joshua did. The gates of Jericho were kept tightly shut because the people were afraid of the Israelis; no one was allowed to go in or out. But the Lord said to Joshua...

Lord   Jericho and its king and all its mighty warriors are already defeated, for I have given them to you! Your entire army is to walk around the city once a day for six days, followed by seven priests walking ahead of the Ark, each carrying a trumpet made from a ram's horn. On the seventh day you are to walk around the city seven times, with the priests blowing their trumpets. Then, when they give one long, loud blast, all the people are to give a mighty shout and the walls of the city will fall down; then move in upon the city from every direction.

Narrator   So Joshua summoned the priests and gave them their instructions; the armed men would lead the procession followed by seven priests blowing continually on their trumpets. Behind them would come the priests carrying the Ark, followed by a rear guard.

Joshua   Let there be complete silence except for the trumpets. Not a single word from any of you until I tell you to shout; then shout!

Narrator   The Ark was carried around the city once that day, after which everyone returned to the camp again and spent the night there. At dawn the next morning they went around again, and returned again to the camp. They followed the pattern for six days. At dawn the seventh day they started out again, but this time they went around the city not once, but seven times. The seventh time, as the priests blew a long, loud trumpet blast, Joshua yelled to the people.

Joshua   Shout! The Lord has given us the city.

Narrator   (He had told them previously, Kill everyone except Rahab the prostitute and anyone in her house, for she protected our spies. Don't take any loot, for everything is to be destroyed. If it isn't, disaster will fall upon the entire nation of Israel. But all the silver and gold and the utensils of bronze and iron will be dedicated to the Lord, and must be brought into his treasury.) So when the people heard the trumpet blast, they shouted as loud as they could. And suddenly the walls of Jericho crumbled and fell before them, and the people of Israel poured into the city from every side and captured it! They destroyed everything in it-men and women, young and old; oxen; sheep; donkeys-everything. Meanwhile Joshua had said to the two spies...

Joshua   Keep your promise. Go and rescue the prostitute and everyone with her.

Narrator   The young men found her and rescued her, along with her father, mother, brothers, and other relatives who were with her. Arrangements were made for them to live outside the camp of Israel. Then the Israelis burned the city and everything in it except the silver and gold and the bronze and iron utensils were kept for the Lord's treasury. Thus Joshua saved Rahab the prostitute and her relatives who were with her in the house, and they still live among the Israelites because she hid the spies sent to Jericho by Joshua. Then Joshua declared a terrible curse upon anyone who might rebuild Jericho, warning that when the foundation was laid, the builder's oldest son would die, and when the gates were set up, his youngest son would die. So the Lord was with Joshua, and his name became famous everywhere.

Samson and Delilah

Judges 16: 1-31 (NLT)

You will need:

Actors	Props
Narrator	7 Bowstrings (strip of leather)
Philistines (one speaking)	Robe
Rulers	Fabric
Delilah	Razor (optional, see tips)
Samson	2 Pillars
Men of Gaza (one speaking)	2 Posts

Tips:

- Use rope or yarn for the bowstrings if leather is not available.
- For safety, use a plastic cutlery knife for a razor.
- Use a knitted cap for Samson to put on to hide his hair.
- Use two students for the pillars.
- Use pool noodles for the posts.

Set the scene:

An angel told Samson's mother that she would have a son and he would be dedicated to God and his hair was never to be cut. He will take the lead in delivering Israel from the hands of the Philistines.

Discussion ideas:

- Samson was a strong man, but he gave into temptation by sharing the secret of his strength with Delilah. She kept asking and asking for his secret. Have you ever been in a situation where you were tempted over and over by the same people? Did you finally give in to the temptation? We can pray and ask God to give us the strength to remain obedient when temptation comes.

- Have you ever heard of the saying, "Bad company corrupts good character?" Samson chose to spend time with someone who valued money over relationships. Delilah was deceitful and betrayed Samson. We need to be careful when choosing whom we spend time with and whom we put our trust in. Ask God to give you wisdom in this area. Good friends will help each other grow in Christ.

Narrator	One day Samson went to the Philistine town of Gaza and spent the night with a prostitute. Word soon spread that Samson was there, so the men of Gaza gathered together and waited all night at the town gates. They kept quiet during the night, saying to themselves...
Men	When the light of morning comes, we will kill him.
Narrator	But Samson stayed in bed only until midnight. Then he got up, took hold of the doors of the town gate, including the two posts, and lifted them up, bar and all. He put them on his shoulders and carried them all the way to the top of the hill across from Hebron. Sometime later Samson fell in love with a woman named Delilah, who lived in the valley of Sorek. The rulers of the Philistines went to her and said...
Ruler	Entice Samson to tell you what makes him so strong and how he can be overpowered and tied up securely. Then each of us will give you 1,100 pieces of silver.
Narrator	So Delilah said to Samson.
Delilah	Please tell me what makes you so strong and what it would take to tie you up securely.
Samson	If I were tied up with seven new bowstrings that have not yet been dried, I would become as weak as anyone else.
Narrator	So the Philistine rulers brought Delilah seven new bowstrings, and she tied Samson up with them. She had hidden some men in one of the inner rooms of her house, and she cried out.
Delilah	Samson! The Philistines have come to capture you!
Narrator	But Samson snapped the bowstrings as a piece of string snaps when it is burned by a fire. So the secret of his strength was not discovered. Afterward Delilah said to him...

Delilah	You've been making fun of me and telling me lies! Now please tell how you can be tied up securely.
Samson	If I were tied up with brand-new ropes that had never been used, I would become as weak as anyone else.
Narrator	So Delilah took new ropes and tied him up with them. The men were hiding in the inner room as before, and again Delilah cried out…
Delilah	Samson! The Philistines have come to capture you!
Narrator	But again Samson snapped the ropes from his arms as if they were thread. Then Delilah said…
Delilah	You've been making fun of me and telling me lies! Now tell me how you can be tied up securely.
Samson	If you were to weave the seven braids of my hair into the fabric on your loom and tighten it with the loom shuttle, I would become as weak as anyone else.
Narrator	So while he slept, Delilah wove the seven braids of his hair into the fabric. Then she tightened it with the loom shuttle. Again she cried out…
Delilah	Samson! The Philistines have come to capture you!
Narrator	But Samson woke up, pulled back the loom shuttle, and yanked his hair away from the loom and the fabric. Then Delilah pouted…
Delilah	How can you tell me, 'I love you,' when you don't share your secrets with me? You've made fun of me three times now, and you still haven't told me what makes you so strong!
Narrator	She tormented him with her nagging day after day until he was sick to death of it. Finally, Samson shared his secret with her.

Samson	My hair has never been cut for I was dedicated to God as a Nazirite from birth. If my head were saved, my strength would leave me, and I would become as weak as anyone else.
Narrator	Delilah realized he had finally told her the truth, so she sent for the Philistine rulers.
Delilah	Come back one more time, for he has finally told me his secret.
Narrator	So the Philistine rulers returned with the money in their hands. Delilah lulled Samson to sleep with his head in her lap, and then she called in a man to shave off the seven locks of his hair. In this way she began to bring him down, and his strength left him.
Delilah	Samson! The Philistines have come to capture you!
Narrator	When he woke up, he thought...
Samson	I will do as before and shake myself free.
Narrator	But he didn't realize the Lord had left him. So the Philistines captured him and gouged out his eyes. They took him to Gaza, where he was bound with bronze chains and forced to grind grain in the prison. But before long, his hair began to grow back. The Philistine rulers held a great festival, offering sacrifices and praising their god, Dagon. They said...
Ruler	Our god has given us victory over our enemy Samson!
Narrator	When the people saw him, they praised their god, saying...
Philistines	Our god has delivered our enemy to us! The one who killed so many of us is now in our power!
Narrator	Half drunk by now, the people demanded...
Philistines	Bring out Samson so he can amuse us!

Narrator	So he was brought from the prison to amuse them, and they had him stand between the pillars supporting the roof. Samson said to the young servant who was leading him by the hand...
Samson	Place my hands against the pillars that hold up the temple. I want to rest against them.
Narrator	Now the temple was completely filled with people. All the Philistine rulers were there, and there were about 3,000 men and women on the roof who were watching as Samson amused them. Then Samson prayed to the Lord...
Samson	Sovereign Lord, remember me again. O God, please strengthen me just one more time. With one blow let me pay back the Philistines for the loss of my two eyes.
Narrator	Then Samson put his hands on the two center pillars that held up the temple. Pushing against them with both hand, he prayed.
Samson	Let me die with the Philistines.
Narrator	And the temple crashed down on the Philistine rulers and all the people. So he killed more people when he died than he had during his entire lifetime. Later his brothers and other relatives went down to get his body. They took him back home and buried him between Zorah and Eshtaol, where his father, Manoah, was buried. Samson had judged Israel for twenty years.

Naomi and Ruth

Ruth 1 (NIV)

You will need:

Actors   Props
    Narrator
    Naomi
    Opah
    Ruth
    Women (one to speak)
    3 Men (Naomi's husband and
        sons) (non-speaking)

Tips:

- Designate an area for Moab and an area for Bethlehem.

Set the scene:

There was a famine in Bethlehem and Naomi and her family fled Bethlehem to go to Moab. Moab was a pagan country of unbelievers.

Discussion Ideas:

- Ruth and Opah were Moabites and Moab was a country of unbelievers, but Naomi must have shared with them about God. Ruth became a believer and said she wanted Naomi's God to be her God. Have you ever had the opportunity to witness to an unbeliever?
- It was a sacrifice for Ruth to return to Bethlehem with Naomi? She was leaving her hometown, and as a Moabite, she would be looked down upon. She loved Naomi and remained faithful to her.
- Naomi had experienced some hardships and was bitter. She lost sight of the resources she had in her relationships with God and with Ruth. When you face bitter times, don't overlook the love and strength from your relationships. Can you think of a time when your friends and family helped you through a trying time? What happened?

Narrator   In the days when the judges ruled, there was a famine in the land. So a man from Bethlehem in Judah, together with his wife and two sons, went to live for a while in the country of Moab. The man's name was Elimelek, his wife's name was Naomi, and the names of his two sons were Mahlon and Kilion. They were Ephrathites from Bethlehem, Judah. And they went to Moab and lived there. Now Elimelek, Naomi's husband, died, and she was left with her two sons. They married Moabite women, one named Orpah and the other Ruth. After they had lived there about ten years, both Mahlon and Kilion also died, and Naomi was left without her two sons and her husband. When Naomi heard in Moab that the Lord had come to the aid of his people by providing food for them, she and her daughters-in-law prepared to return home from there. With her two daughters-in-law she left the place where she had been living and set out on the road that would take them back to the land of Judah. Then Naomi said to her two daughters-in-law...

Naomi   Go back, each of you, to your mother's home. May the Lord show you, kindness, as you have shown kindness to your dead husbands and to me. May the Lord grant that each of you will find rest in the home of another husband.

Narrator   Then she kissed them goodbye and they wept aloud and said to her...

Orpah   We will go back with you to your people.

Naomi   Return home, my daughters. Why would you come with me? Am I going to have any more sons, who could become your husbands? Return home, my daughters; I am too old to have another husband. Even if I thought there was still hope for me—even if I had a husband tonight and then gave birth to sons—would you wait until they grew up? Would you remain unmarried for them? No, my daughters. It is more bitter for me than for you, because the Lord's hand has turned against me!

Narrator   At this they wept aloud again. Then Orpah kissed her mother-in-law goodbye, but Ruth clung to her.

Naomi   Look, your sister-in-law is going back to her people and her gods. Go back with her.

Ruth   Don't urge me to leave you or to turn back from you. Where you go I will go, and where you stay I will stay. Your people will be my people and your God my God. Where you die I will die, and there I will be buried. May the Lord deal with me, be it ever so severely, if even death separates you and me.

Narrator   When Naomi realized that Ruth was determined to go with her, she stopped urging her. So the two women went on until they came to Bethlehem. When they arrived in Bethlehem, the whole town was stirred because of them, and the women exclaimed...

Women   Can this be Naomi?

Naomi   Don't call me Naomi. Call me Mara, because the Almighty has made my life very bitter. I went away full, but the Lord has brought me back empty. Why call me Naomi? The Lord has afflicted me; the Almighty has brought misfortune upon me.

Narrator   So Naomi returned from Moab accompanied by Ruth the Moabite, her daughter-in-law, arriving in Bethlehem as the barley harvest was beginning.

Samuel Anoints David

1 Samuel 16: 1-13 (ESV)

You will need:

Actors	Props
Narrator	Drinking horn
Lord	
Samuel	
Jesse	
Elders (one speaking)	
David (non-speaking)	
Eliah, Abinadab, Shammah, & 4 other brothers (non-speaking)	

Tips:

- Create an area for both Samuel's house and Jesse's house. Designate an area for the field away from Jesse's so they can go get David to bring him back.
- Make a horn from construction paper.

Set the scene:

Saul was the previous king, but he was rejected by the Lord. Now, God is ready to anoint a new king.

Discussion Idea:

- Why do you think God told Samuel not to consider appearance? Saul, the previous king, was tall and impressive looking. David was the youngest of Jesse's sons and not very big in size, but, God knew his heart. We need to remember to see people for what they are on the inside and not their outward appearances.

- A person's character is more important than his/her outward appearance. When you choose friends, is it more important that they are attractive and wear fashionable clothes or do you look for character traits such as kindness and honesty?

- Do you ever feel like God can't use you because you are young and not very important? David was the youngest of his brothers and only a shepherd. They didn't think he was important enough or strong enough to be a king, but God had big plans for David. God saw David's heart.

Narrator   The Lord said to Samuel.

Lord   How long will you grieve over Saul, since I have ejected him from being king over Israel? Fill your horn with oil, and go. I will send you to Jesse the Bethlehemite, for I have provided for myself a king among his sons.

Samuel   How can I go? If Saul hears it, he will kill me.

Lord   Take a heifer with you and say, 'I have come to sacrifice to the Lord.' And invite Jesse to the sacrifice, and I will show you what you shall do. And you shall anoint for me him whom I declare to you.

Narrator   Samuel did what the Lord commanded and came to Bethlehem. The elders of the city came to meet him trembling and said...

Elders   Do you come peaceably?

Samuel   Peaceably; I have come to sacrifice to the Lord. Consecrate yourselves, and come with me to the sacrifice.

Narrator   And he consecrated Jesse and his sons and invited them to the sacrifice. When they came, he looked on Eliab and thought, Surely the Lord's anointed is before him. But the Lord said to Samuel...

Lord   Do not look on his appearance or on the height of his statue, because I have rejected him. For the Lord sees not as man sees; man looks on the outward appearance, but the Lord looks on the heart.

Narrator   Then Jesse called Abinadab and made him pass before Samuel. And he said...

Samuel   Neither has the Lord chosen this one.

Narrator   And Jesse made Shammah pass by. And Samuel said...

Samuel   Neither has the Lord chosen this one.

Narrator   And Jesse made seven of his sons pass before Samuel. And Samuel said...

Samuel   The Lord has not chosen these. Are all your sons here?

Jesse   There remains yet the youngest, but behold, he is keeping the sheep.

Samuel   Send and get him, for we will not sit down till he comes here.

Narrator   And he sent and brought him in. Now he was ruddy and had beautiful eyes and was handsome. And the Lord said...

Lord   Arise, anoint him, for this is he.

Narrator   Then Samuel took the horn of oil and anointed him in the midst of his brothers. And the Spirit of the Lord rushed upon David from that day forward. And Samuel rose up and went to Ramah.

David and Goliath
1 Samuel 17 (ESV)

You will need:

Actors   Props

    Narrator   2 Swords

    Goliath   Sling shot

    Philistine   5 Stones

    King Saul   Pouch

    David   King's armor

    Jesse   Basket (for food)

    Eliab (Brother to David)

    Israelites (one speaking)

    Abner

Tips:

- Create a setting that represents two hills separated by a valley, one for the Israelites and one for the Philistines.
- Use ping pong balls instead of stones.
- Use heavy coats for the king's armor.
- Use an empty box for the actors to pretend to put Goliath's head in to carry around.

Set the scene:

The Philistines wanted to fight the Israelites to gain control of their land.

Discussion ideas:

- Do you ever feel like you have to be someone that you are not in order to be a good Christian? David chose not to wear the King's armor because it felt cumbersome and unfamiliar. He was more comfortable with his simple slingshot. Every time he had used his slingshot to protect his sheep, he was being prepared for this future battle with Goliath. God will use the unique skills He's already placed in your hands, so don't worry about trying to be someone else. Just be yourself and use the familiar gifts and talents God has given you.

- Are you facing any giants right now? It might not be a physical giant, but maybe a subject in school you are having trouble with or you're being picked on by the bullies at school . You might feel like you don't have what it takes to face your situation, but remember that David didn't seem equipped for his situation either. He trusted God to help him and you can trust God too.

| Narrator | Now the Philistines gathered their armies for battle. And they were gathered at Socoh, which belongs to Judah, and encamped between Socoh and Azekah, in Ephes-dammim. And Saul and the men of Israel were gathered, and encamped in the valley of Elah, and drew up in line of battle against the Philistines. And the Philistines stood on the mountain on the one side, and Israel stood on the mountain on the other side, with a valley between them. And there came out from the camp of the Philistines a champion named Goliath of Gath, whose height was six cubits and a span. He had a helmet of bronze on his head, and he was armed with a coat of mail, and the weight of the coat was five thousand shekels of bronze. And he had bronze armor on his legs, and a javelin of bronze slung between his shoulders. The shaft of his spear was like a weaver's beam, and his spear's head weighed six hundred shekels of iron. And his shield-bearer went before him. He stood and shouted to the ranks of Israel. |

| Goliath | Why have you come out to draw up for battle? Am I not a Philistine, and are you not servants of Saul? Choose a man for yourselves, and let him come down to me. If he is able to fight with me and kill me, then we will be your servants. But if I prevail against him and kill him, then you shall be our servants and serve us. |

| Philistine | I defy the ranks of Israel this day. Give me a man, that we may fight together. |

| Narrator | When Saul and all Israel heard these words of the Philistine, they were dismayed and greatly afraid. Now David was the son of an Ephrathite of Bethlehem in Judah, named Jesse, who had eight sons. In the days of Saul the man was already old and advanced in year. The three oldest sons of Jesse had followed Saul to the battle. And the names of his three sons who went to the battle were Eliab the firstborn, and next to him Abinadab, and the third Shammah. David was the youngest. The three eldest followed Saul, but David went back and forth from Saul to feed his father's sheep at Bethlehem. For forty days the Philistine came forward and took his stand, morning and evening. And Jesse said to David's his son... |

| Jesse | Take for your bothers and Ephah of this parched grain, and these ten loaves, and carry them quickly to the camp to your brothers. Also take these ten cheeses to the commander of their thousand. See if your brothers are well, and bring some token from them. |

Narrator   Now Saul and they and all the men of Israel were in the Valley of Elah, fighting with the Philistines. And David rose early in the morning and left the sheep with a keeper and took the provisions and sent, as Jesse had commanded him. And he came to the encampment as the host was going out to the battle line, shouting the war cry. And Israel and the Philistines drew up for battle, army against army. And David left the things in charge of the keeper of the baggage and ran to the ranks and went and greeted his brothers. As he talked with them, behold, the champion, the Philistine of Gath, Goliath by name, came up out of the ranks of the Philistines and spoke the same words as before. And David heard him. All the men of Israel, when they saw the man, fled from him and were much afraid. And the men of Israel said...

Israelites   Have you seen this man who has come up? Surely he has come up to defy Israel. And the king will enrich the man who kills him with great riches and will give him his daughter and make his father's house free in Israel.

David   What shall be done for the man who kills this Philistine and takes away the reproach from Israel? For who is this uncircumcised Philistine, that he should defy the armies of the living God?

Narrator   And the people answered him in the same way.

Israelites   So shall it be done to the man who kills him.

Narrator   Now Eliab his eldest brother heard when he spoke to the men. And Eliab's anger was kindled against David and he said...

Eliab   Why have you come down? And with whom have you left those few sheep in the wilderness? I know your presumption and the evil of your heart, for you have come down to see the battle.

David   What have I done now? Was it not but a word?

Narrator   And he turned away from him toward another, and spoke in the same way, and the people answered him again as before. When the words that David spoke were heard, they repeated them before Saul, and he sent for him. And David said to Saul...

David   Let no man's heart fail because of him. Your servant will go and fight with this Philistine.

Saul   You are not able to go against this Philistine to fight with him, for you are but a youth, and he has been a man of war from his youth.

David   Your servant used to keep sheep for his father. And when there came a lion, or a bear, and took a lamb from the flock. I went after him and struck him and delivered it out of his mouth. And if he arose against me, I caught him by his beard and struck him and killed him. Your servant has struck down both lions and bears, and this uncircumcised Philistine shall be like one of them, for he has defied the armies of the living God. The Lord who delivered me from the paw of the lion and from the paw of the bear will deliver me from the hand of this Philistine.

Saul   Go, and the Lord be with you!

Narrator Then Saul clothed David with his armor. He put a helmet of bronze on his head and clothed him with a coat of mail, and David strapped his sword over his armor. And he tried in vain to go, for he had not tested them. Then David said to Saul...

David   I cannot go with these, for I have not tested them.

Narrator So David put them off. Then he took his staff in his hand and chose five smooth stones from the brook and put them in his shepherd's pouch. His sling was in his hand, and approached the Philistine. And the Philistine moved forward and came near to David, with his shield-bearer in front of him. And when the Philistine looked and saw David, he disdained him, for he was but a youth, ruddy and handsome in appearance. And the Philistine said to David...

Goliath   Am I a dog, that you come to me with sticks?

Narrator   And the Philistine cursed David by his gods. The Philistine said to David...

Goliath   Come to me, and I will give your flesh to the birds of the air and to the beasts of the field.

David   You come to me with a sword and with a spear and with a javelin, but I come to you in the name of the Lord of hosts, the God of the armies of Israel, whom you have defied. This day the Lord will deliver you into my hand, and I will strike you down and cut off your head. And I will give the dead bodies of the host of the Philistines this day to the birds of the air and to the wild beasts of the earth, that all the earth may know that there is a God in Israel and that all this assembly may know that the Lord saves not with sword and spear. For the battle is the Lord's, and he will give you into our hand.

Narrator   When the philistine arose and came and drew near to meet David, David ran quickly toward the battle line to meet the Philistine. And David put his hand in his bag and took out a stone and slung it and struck the Philistine on his forehead. The stone sank into his forehead, and he fell on his face to the ground. So David prevailed over the Philistine with a sling and with a stone, and struck the Philistine and killed him. There was no sword in the hand of David. Then David ran and stood over the Philistine and took his sword and drew it out of its sheath and killed him and cut off his head with it. When the Philistines saw that their champion was dead, they fled. And the men of Israel and Judah rose with a shout and pursued the Philistines as far as Gath and the gates of Ekron, so that the wounded Philistines fell on the way from Shaaraim as far as Gath and Ekron. And the people of Israel came back from chasing the Philistines, and they plundered their camp. And David took the head of the Philistine and brought it to Jerusalem, but he put his armor in his tent. As soon as Saul saw David go out against the Philistine, he said Abner, the commander of the army, 'Abner, whose son is this youth?' And Abner said...

Abner   As your soul lives, O king, I do not know.

Saul   Inquire whose son the boy is.

Narrator   And as soon as David returned from the striking down of the Philistine, Abner took him, and brought him before Saul with the head of the Philistine in his hand. And Saul said to him...

Saul   Whose son are you, young man?

David   I am the son of your servant Jesse the Bethlehemite.

David, Nabal and Abigail

1 Samuel 25: 1-42 (TLB)

You will need:

Actor   Props

    Narrator   Basket of food

    David   Swords

    Nabal

    Servant

    Abigail

    10 Young men (one speaking)

Tip:

- Designate an area for Abigail's house in Carmel and an area for the wilderness.

Set the scene:

Samuel died and David, who had been anointed by Samuel to be king, moved to the wilderness.

Discussion ideas:

- David was ready to kill Nabal, but he took the time to listen to Abigail. Even when we think we are right, we should always stop to listen to what others have to say. Can you think of a time when you listened to others and it kept you from making a mistake? What happened?
- Nabal was harsh and rude towards others, but Abigail was a peacemaker. When she found out that Nabal had offended David, she went to David to try to resolve the conflict. She saved lives that day. Think about how you interact with others. Are you harsh and cause conflict, or are you a peacemaker? Which one brings honor to God?

Narrator	Shortly afterwards, Samuel died and all Israel gathered for his funeral and buried him in his family plot at Ramah. Meanwhile David went down to the wilderness to Paran. A wealthy man from Maon owned a sheep ranch there, near the village of Carmel. He had three thousand sheep and a thousand goats, and was at his ranch at this time for the sheep shearing. His name was Nabal and his wife, a beautiful and very intelligent woman, was named Abigail. But the man, who was a descendant of Caleb, was uncouth, churlish, stubborn, and ill-mannered. When David heard that Nabal was shearing his sheep, he sent ten of his young men to Carmel to give him this message...
David	May God prosper you and your family and multiply everything you own. I am told that you are shearing your sheep and goats. While your shepherds have lived among us, we have never harmed them, nor stolen anything from them the whole time they have been in Carmel. Ask your young men and they will tell you whether or not this is true. Now I have sent my men to ask for a little contribution from you, for we have come at a happy time of holiday. Please give us a present of whatever is at hand.
Narrator	The young men gave David's message to Nabal and waited for his reply.
Nabal	Who is this fellow David? Who does this son of Jesse think he is? There are lots of servants these days who run away from their masters. Should I take my bread and my water and my meat that I've slaughtered for my shearers and give it to a gang who comes from God knows where?
Narrator	So David's messengers returned and told him what Nabal had said.
David	Get your swords!
Narrator	Four hundred of them started off with David and two hundred remained behind to guard their gear. Meanwhile, one of Nabal's men went and told Abigail.
Men	David sent men from the wilderness to talk to our master, but he insulted them and railed at them. But David's men were very good to us and we never suffered any harm from them; in fact, day and night they were like a wall of protection to us and the sheep, and nothing was stolen from us the whole

time they were with us. You'd better think fast, for there is going to be trouble for our master and his whole family-he's such a stubborn lout that no one can even talk to him!

Narrator   Then Abigail hurriedly took two hundred loaves of bread, two barrels of wine, five dressed sheep, two bushels of roasted grain, one hundred raisin cakes, and two hundred fig cakes, and packed them onto donkeys.

Abigail   Go on ahead and I will follow.

Narrator   But she didn't tell her husband what she was doing. As she was riding down the trail on her donkey, she met David coming towards her. David had been saying to himself.

David   A lot of good it did us to help this fellow. We protected his flocks in the wilderness so that not one thing was lost or stolen, but he had repaid me bad for good. All that I get for my trouble is insults. May God curse me if even one of his men remains alive by tomorrow morning!

Narrator   When Abigail saw David, she quickly dismounted and bowed low before him.

Abigail   I accept all blame in this matter, my lord. Please listen to what I want to say. Nabal is a bad-tempered boor, but please don't pay any attention to what he said. He is a fool-just like his name means. But I didn't see the messengers you sent. Sir, since the Lord has kept you from murdering and taking vengeance into your own hands, I pray by the life of God, and by your own life too, that all your enemies shall be as cursed as Nabal is. And now, here is a present I have brought to you and your young men. Forgive me for my boldness in coming out here. The Lord will surely reward you with eternal royalty for your descendants, for you are fighting his battles; and you will never do wrong throughout your entire life. Even when you are chased by those who seek your life, you are safe in the care of the Lord your God, just as though you were safe inside his purse! But the lives of your enemies shall disappear like stones from a sling! When the Lord has done all the good things he promised you and has made you king of Israel, you won't want the conscience of a murderer who took the law into his own hands! And when the Lord has done these great things for you, please remember me!

David   Bless the Lord God of Israel who has sent you to meet me today! Thank God for your good sense! Bless you for keeping me from murdering the man and carrying out vengeance with my own hands. For I swear by the Lord, the God of Israel who has kept me from hurting you, that if you had not come out to meet me, not one of Nabal's men would be alive tomorrow morning.

Narrator   Then David accepted her gifts and told her to return home without fear, for he would not kill her husband. When she arrived home she found that Nabal had thrown a big party. He was roaring drunk, so she didn't tell him anything about her meeting with David until the next morning. By that time he was sober, and when his wife told him what had happened, he had a stroke and lay paralyzed for about ten days, then died, for the Lord killed him. When David heard that Nabal was dead, he said...

David   Praise the Lord! God has paid back Nabal and kept me from doing it myself; he has received his punishment for his sin.

Narrator   Then David wasted no time in sending messengers to Abigail to ask her to become his wife. When the messengers arrived at Carmel and told her why they had come, she readily agreed to his request. Quickly getting ready, she took along five of her serving girls as attendants, mounted her donkey, and followed the men back to David. So she became his wife.

David and Bathsheba

2 Samuel 11:1 – 12:14 (TLB)

You will need:

Actors	Props
Narrator	2 Roofs
Nathan	Letter
David	
Bathsheba	
Uriah	
Messenger	
Servant	
Joab	

Tips:

- Use tables for the roofs, one for David and one for Bathsheba.

Set the scene:

David sent his army out to war, but David did not go. He stayed in Jerusalem.

Discussion ideas:

- David allowed himself to fall deeper and deeper into sin. He gave into his desires and temptations. He sinned deliberately and then tried to cover it up by deceiving others. He then committed murder to continue the cover-up. Can you think of any examples in your life of one sin leading to others? When you realize that there is sin in your life, the best solution is to deal with before it grows. Pray and ask God to help you with your situation.

- We learn at the end of this story that David was forgiven for his sins, however there would be serious consequences for his actions. When we seek forgiveness for our sins, God certainly forgives us. But, often there are consequences for our actions. Remember this when temptation comes along and ask God to help you remain faithful and obedient to His will.

Narrator   In the spring of the following year, at the time when wars begin, David sent Joab and the Israeli army to destroy the Ammonites. They began by laying siege to the city of Rabbah. But David stayed in Jerusalem. One night he couldn't get to sleep and went for a stroll on the roof of the palace. As he looked out over the city, he noticed a woman of unusual beauty taking her evening bath. He sent to find out who she was and was told that she was Bath-sheba, the daughter of Eliam and the wife of Uriah. Then David sent for her and when she came he slept with her. (She had just completed the purification rites after menstruation.) Then she returned home. When she found that he had gotten her pregnant she sent a message to inform him.

Narrator   So David dispatched a memo to Joab: "Send me Uriah the Hittite." When he arrived, David asked him how Joab and the army were getting along and how the war was prospering. Then he told him to go home and relax, and he sent a present to him at his home. But Uriah didn't go there. He stayed that night at the gateway of the palace with the other servants of the king. When David heard what Uriah had done, he summoned him and asked him.

David   What's the matter with you? Why didn't you go home to your wife last night after being away for so long?

Uriah   The Ark and the armies and the general and his officers are camping out in open fields, and should I go home to wine and dine and sleep with my wife? I swear that I will never be guilty of acting like that.

David   Well, stay here tonight, and tomorrow you may return to the army.

Narrator   So Uriah stayed around the palace. David invited him to dinner and got him drunk; but even so he didn't go home that night, but again he slept at the entry to the palace. Finally the next morning David wrote a letter to Joab and gave it to Uriah to deliver. The letter instructed Joab to put Uriah at the front of the hottest part of the battle-and then pull back and leave him there to die! So Joab assigned Uriah to a spot close to the besieged city where he knew that the enemies best men were fighting: and Uriah was killed along with several other Israeli soldiers. When Joab sent a report to David of how the battle was going, he told his messenger.

Joab	If the king is angry and asks, 'Why did the troops go to close to the city? Didn't they know there would be shooting from the walls? Wasn't Abimelech killed at Thebez by a woman who threw down a millstone on him?-then tell him, Uriah was killed, too.
Narrator	So the messenger arrived at Jerusalem, and gave the report to David.
Messenger	The enemy came out against us, and as we chased them back to the city gates, the men on the wall attacked us; and some of our men were killed, and Uriah the Hittite is dead too.
David	Well, tell Joab not to be discouraged. The sword kills one as well as another! Fight harder next time, and conquer the city; tell him he is doing well.
Narrator	When Bath-sheba heard that her husband was dead, she mourned for him; then, when the period of mourning was over, David sent for her and brought her to the palace and she became one of his wives; and she gave birth to his son. But the Lord was very displeased with what David had done. So the Lord sent the prophet Nathan to tell David this story..
Nathan	There were two men in a certain city, one very rich, owning many flocks of sheep and herds of goats; and the other very poor, owning nothing but a little lamb he had managed to buy. It was his children's pet and he fed it from his own plate and let it drink from his own cup; he cuddled it in his arms like a baby daughter. Recently a guest arrived at the home of the rich man. But instead of killing a lamb from his own flocks for food for the traveler, he took the poor man's lamb and roasted it and served it. David was furious.
David	I swear by the living God, any man who would do a thing like that should be put to death; he shall repay four lambs to the poor man for the one he stole, and for having no pity.
Nathan	You are that rich man! The Lord God of Israel says, 'I made you king of Israel and saved you from the power of Saul. I gave you his palace and his wives and the kingdoms of Israel and Judah; and if that had not been enough, I would have given you much, much more. Why, then have you despised the laws of

God and done this horrible deed? For you have murdered Uriah and stolen his wife. Therefore murder shall be a constant threat in your family from this time on, because you have insulted me by taking Uriah's wife. I vow that because of what you have done I will cause your own household to rebel against you. I will give your wives to another man, and he will go to bed with them in public view. You did it secretly, but I will do this to you openly, in the sight of all Isreal

David   I have sinned against the Lord.

Nathan   Yes, but the Lord has forgiven you, and you won't die for this sin. But you have given great opportunity to the enemies of the Lord to despise and blaspheme him, so your child shall die.

Solomon Asks for Wisdom

1 Kings 3: 1-28 (TLB)

You will need:

Actors   Props

    Narrator   Bed (for Solomon)

    Solomon   Burnt Offerings

    God   Baby (2)

    Woman 1   Sword

    Woman 2

Tips:

- Create an area for Jerusalem and an area for Gibeon.
- Put a sheet over a table for Solomon's bed.

Set the scene:

David had reigned over Israel for 40 years. Just before David died, he gave a charge to Solomon, his son, to walk in the ways of the Lord. At David's death, Solomon took the throne to rule over Israel.

Discussion ideas:

- If you could ask God for anything, what would it be? Would you ask for material things? Would you ask for Power? Or, would you ask for wisdom, like Solomon?
- Did Solomon ask for wisdom so he could become more powerful than everyone? Notice his attitude of thankfulness and humility as he asks God for wisdom. He wasn't asking for wisdom to make himself more powerful, but so that he could better serve his people. God blesses us when we seek to serve others. Ask God to show you how you can better serve others. Ask Him to give you wisdom as you seek to obey His will.

Narrator   Solomon made an alliance with Pharoah, the king of Egypt, and married one of his daughters. He brought her to Jerusalem to live in the City of David until he could finish building his palace and the Temple, and the wall around the city. At that time the people of Israel sacrificed their offerings on altars in the hills, for the Temple of the Lord hadn't yet been build. (Solomon loved the Lord and followed all of his father David's instructions except that he continued to sacrifice in the hills and to offer incense there.) The most famous of the hilltop altars was at Gibeon and now the king went there and sacrificed one thousand burnt offerings! The Lord appeared to him in a dream that night and told him to ask for anything he wanted, and it would be given to him! Solomon replied.

Solomon   You were wonderfully kind to my father David because he was honest and true and faithful to you, and obeyed your commands. And you have continued your kindness to him by giving him a son to succeed him. O Lord my God, now you have made me the king instead of my father David, but I am as a little child who doesn't know his way around. And here I am among your own chosen people, a nation so great that there are almost too many people to count! Give me an understanding mind so that I can govern your people well and know the difference between what is right and what is wrong. For who by himself is able to carry such a heavy responsibility?

Narrator   The Lord was pleased with his reply and was glad that Solomon had asked for wisdom. So he replied...

God   Because you have asked for wisdom in governing my people and haven't asked for a long life or riches for yourself, or the defeat of your enemies-yes, I'll give you what you asked for! I will give you a wiser mind than anyone else has ever had or ever will have! And I will also give you what you didn't ask for-riches and honor! And no one in all the world will be as rich and famous as you for the rest of your life! And I will give you a long life it you follow me and obey my laws as your father David did.

Narrator   Then Solomon woke up and realized it had been a dream. He returned to Jerusalem and went into the Tabernacle. And as he stood before the Ark of the Covenant of the Lord, he sacrificed burnt offerings and peace offerings. Then he invited all of his officials to a great banquet. Soon afterwards two young prostitutes came to the king to have an argument settled.

Woman 1   Sir, we live in the same house, just the two of us, and recently I had a baby. When it was three days old, this woman's baby was born too. But her baby died during the night when she rolled over it in her sleep and smothered it. Then she got up in the night and took my son from beside me while I was asleep, and laid her dead child in my arms and took mine to sleep beside her. And in the morning when I tried to feed my baby it was dead! But when it became light outside, I saw that it wasn't my son at all.

Woman 2   It certainly was her son, and the living child is mine.

Woman 1   No, the dead one is yours and the living one is mine.

Narrator   And so they argued back and forth before the king. Then the king said...

Solomon   Let's get the facts straight; both of you claim the living child, and each says that the dead child belongs to the other. All right, bring me a sword..

Narrator   So a sword was brought to the king. Then he said...

Solomon   Divide the living child in two and give half to each of these women!

Narrator   Then the woman who really was the mother of the child, and who loved him very much, cried out.

Woman 1   Oh, no, sir! Give her the child-don't kill him!

Woman 2   All right, it will be neither yours nor mine; divide it between us!

Solomon   Give the baby to the woman who wants him to live, for she is the mother!

Narrator   Word of the king's decision spread quickly throughout the entire nation, and all the people were awed as they realized the great wisdom God had given him.

Elijah and the Widow

1 Kings 17:8 -24 (ESV)

You will need:

Actors	Props
Narrator	Cup
God	Flour
Elijah	Doll
Widow	Bed
Sticks	

Tips:

- Designate an area for the brook and an area for Zarephath with the widow's house.
- The scene opens with Elijah by a brook. Use a blue sheet for the brook and have a cup for Elijah to get water from the brook.
- Use a table for the bed.

Set the scene:

Elijah was a great prophet. God told Elijah to go and hide in a ravine near the Jordan River. God told him to drink from the brook and that He would send the ravens to feed him. Elijah followed God's directions and the ravens brought him bread and meat in the morning and in the evening. But, now there was a drought and the brook was drying up.

Discussion ideas:

- The widow was sure she and her son were going to die because of the drought. How do you think she felt when Elijah told her that God would not allow her flour and oil to be used up? How about several days later when there was still oil and flour? Have you ever witnessed a miracle? (Something you couldn't explain.) If so, how did it affect you?

- The people in Zarephath worshipped Baal, so the widow was unlikely to be a believer in Christ. Doesn't it seem odd that God would use her to meet the need of Elijah? God used the unbeliever to meet Elijah's need and used Elijah to show God's power to the unbeliever. Isn't our God amazing? God provided for both Elijah and the widow, and He will provide for your needs as well.

Narrator	The word of the Lord came to him.
God	Arise, go to Zarephath, which belongs to Sidon, and dwell there. Behold, I have commanded a widow there to feed you. So he arose and went to Zarephath. And when he came to the gate of the city, behold, a widow was there gathering sticks. And he called to her and said...
Elijah	Bring me a little water in a vessel, that I may drink.
Narrator	And as she was going to bring it, he called to her and said...
Elijah	Bring me a morsel of bread in your hand.
Widow	As the Lord your God lives, I have nothing baked, only a handful of flour in a jar and a little oil in a jug. And now I am gathering a couple of sticks that I may go in and prepare it for myself and my son, that we may eat it and die.
Elijah	Do not fear; go and do as you have said. But first make me a little cake of it and bring it to me, and afterward make something for yourself and your son. For thus says the Lord, the God of Israel, 'The jar of flour shall not be spent, and the jug of oil shall not be empty, until the day that the Lord sends rain upon the earth.'
Narrator	And she went and did as Elijah said. And she and he and her household ate for many days. The jar of flour was not spent, neither did the jug of oil become empty, according to the word of the Lord that he spoke by Elijah. After this the son of the woman, the mistress of the house, became ill. And his illness was so severe that there was no breath left in him. And she said to Elijah...
Widow	What have you against me, O man of God? You have come to me to bring my sin to remembrance and to cause the death of my son!
Elijah	Give me your son.
Narrator	And he took him from her arms and carried him up into the upper chamber where he lodged, and laid him on his own bed. And he cried to the Lord...

Elijah   O Lord my God, have you brought calamity even upon the widow with whom I sojourn, by killing her son?

Narrator   Then he stretched himself upon the child three times and cried to the Lord...

Elijah   O Lord my God, let this child's life come into him again.

Narrator   And the Lord listened to the voice of Elijah. And the life of the child came into him again, and he revived. And Elijah took the child and brought him down from the upper chamber into the house and delivered him to his mother. And Elijah said...

Elijah   See, your son lives.

Woman   Now I know that you are a man of God, and that the word of the Lord in your mouth is truth.

Elijah and the Prophets of Baal

1 Kings 18: 17-40 (ESV)

You will need:

Actors

    Narrator

    Elijah

    Ahab

    People

    Swords

    Stuffed animals (bulls)

Props

    2 Tables

    12 Stones

    Wood or sticks

    4 water bottles or jars

Tips:

- Use tables and enough wood or sticks to create a "fire", leaving enough room to surround the wood of one fire with the 12 stones. Use a flashlight or add flames cut from orange and yellow paper to make Elijah's wood burn. Assign a student to add the "fire" at just the right time.
- Use stuffed animals to represent the bulls, or print pictures of one.
- Bring a picture of Baal to show the students what the Canaanites were worshiping. Get this from internet.

Set the scene:

Ahab was the king of Israel. Instead of worshiping God, he and his wife Jezebel were worshiping Baal, the most popular Canaanite god. The Lord told Elijah to go and present himself to Ahab.

Discussion ideas:

- God told Elijah to go to a place where everyone was worshiping other Gods. Can you imagine being the only person around that believes in God? How do you think missionaries feel that go to parts of the world where most people worship other gods or no god at all?

- God will make resources available to us to accomplish what He calls us to do. It may not be as dramatic as a miraculous fire. It may be the courage to stand for truth or the means to provide for someone in need. Have you ever felt God leading you to do something then realized that He gave you exactly what you needed to do it.?

Narrator	When Ahab saw Elijah, Ahab said to him...
Ahab	Is it you, you troubler of Israel?
Elijah	I have not troubled Israel, but you have, and your father's house, because you have abandoned the commandments of the Lord and followed the Baals. Now therefore send and gather all Israel to me at Mount Carmel, and the 450 prophets of Baal and the 400 Prophets of Asherah, who eat at Jezebel's table.
Narrator	So Ahab sent to all the people of Israel and gathered the prophets together at Mount Carmel. And Elijah came near to all the people and said...
Elijah	How long will you go limping between two different opinions? If the Lord is God, follow him; but if Baal, then follow him.
Narrator	And the people did not answer him a word. Then Elijah said to the people...
Elijah	I, even I only, am left a prophet of the Lord, but Baal's prophets are 450 men. Let two bulls be given to us, and let them choose one bull for themselves and cut it in pieces and lay it on the wood, but put no fire to it. And I will prepare the other bull and lay it on the wood and put no fire to it. And you call upon the name of your god, and I will call upon the name of the Lord, and the God who answers by fire, he is God.
Narrator	And all the people answered.
People	It is well spoken.
Narrator	Then Elijah said to the prophets of Baal...
Elijah	Choose for yourselves one bull and prepare it first, for you are many, and call upon the name of your god, but put no fire to it.
Narrator	And they took the bull that was given them, and they prepared it and called upon the name of Baal from morning until noon, saying...

People   O Baal, answer us!

Narrator   But there was no voice, and no one answered. And they limped around the altar that they had made. And at noon Elijah mocked them, saying...

Elijah   Cry aloud, for he is a god. Either he is musing, or he is relieving himself, or he is on a journey, or perhaps he is asleep and must be awakened.

Narrator   And they cried aloud and cut themselves after their custom with swords and lances, until the blood gushed out upon them And as midday passed, they raved on until the time of the offering of the oblation, but there was no voice. No one answered; no one paid attention. Then Elijah said to all the people...

Elijah   Come near to me.

Narrator   And all the people came near to him. And he repaired the altar of the Lord that had been thrown down. Elijah took twelve stones, according to the number of the tribes of the sons of Jacob, to whom the word of the Lord came, saying, "Israel shall be your name, and with the stones he built an altar in the name of the Lord. And he made a trench about the altar, as great as would contain two seahs of seed. And he put the wood in order and cut the bull in pieces and laid it on the wood. And he said...

Elijah   Fill four jars with water and pour it on the burnt offering and on the wood.

Narrator   And he said...

Elijah   Do it a second time.

Narrator   And they did it a second time, and he said...

Elijah   Do it a third time.

Narrator   And the water ran around the altar and filled the trench also with water. And at the time of the offering of the oblation, Elijah the prophet came near and said...

Elijah   O Lord, God of Abraham, Isaac, and Israel, let it be known this day that you are God in Israel, and that I am your servant, and that I have done all these things at your word. Answer me, O Lord, answer me, that this people may know that you, O Lord, are God, and that you have turned their hearts back.

Narrator   Then the fire of the Lord fell and consumed the burnt offering and the wood and the stones and the dust, and licked up the water that was in the trench. And when all the people saw it, they fell on their faces and said...

People   The Lord, he is God; the Lord, he is God.

Elijah   Seize the prophets of Baal; let not one of them escape.

Narrator   And they seized them. And Elijah bought them down to the brook Kishon and slaughtered them there.

Elijah Taken Up to Heaven

2 Kings 2:1-18 (NIV)

You will need:

Actors

    Narrator

    Elijah

    Elisha

    Company (many people,
       one speaking)

Props

    Jordan River

    Cloak

    Clothes

    Chariot of fire (see tips)

Tips:

- Designate areas for Gilgal, Bethel, Jericho, and the Jordan River.
- Use a blue sheet for the Jordan River. If the sheet can be cut, you can have students separate the material to simulate the water parting.
- Use a jacket or robe for a cloak.
- Allow a student to be the Chariot of Fire and come between Elijah and Elisha carrying flames cut from red, orange, and yellow paper.

Set the scene:

Elijah was a great prophet and Elisha was to become his successor as a prophet of God.

Discussion ideas:

- Elisha asked for a double portion of Elijah's spirit. Was that a bold request? God granted his request because Elisha's motives were pure. He did not want to be better or more powerful than Elijah, but wanted to accomplish more for God. Have you ever asked God for a bold request? Were your motives pure? What happened?

Narrator	When the LORD was about to take Elijah up to heaven in a whirlwind, Elijah and Elisha were on their way from Gilgal. Elijah said to Elisha...
Elijah	Stay here; the LORD has sent me to Bethel.
Elisha	As surely as the LORD lives and as you live, I will not leave you.
Narrator	So they went down to Bethel. The company of the prophets at Bethel came out to Elisha and asked...
Company	Do you know that the LORD is going to take your master from you today?
Elisha	Yes, I know, so be quiet.
Elijah	Stay here, Elisha; the LORD has sent me to Jericho.
Elisha	As surely as the LORD lives and as you live, I will not leave you.
Narrator	So they went to Jericho. The Company of the prophets at Jericho went up to Elisha and asked him...
Company	Do you know that the LORD is going to take your master from you today?
Elisha	Yes, I know, so be quiet.
Elijah	Stay here; the LORD has sent me to the Jordan.
Elisha	As surely as the Lord lives and as you live, I will not leave you.
Narrator	So the two of them walked on. Fifty men of the company of the prophets went and stood at a distance, facing the place where Elijah and Elisha had stopped at the Jordan. Elijah took his cloak, rolled it up and struck the water with it. The water divided to the right and to the left, and the two of them crossed over on dry ground. When they had crossed, Elijah said to Elisha...

Elijah	Tell me, what can I do for you before I am taken from you?
Elisha	Let me inherit a double portion of your spirit.
Elijah	You have asked a difficult thing. Yet if you see me when I am taken from you, it will be yours—otherwise, it will not.
Narrator	As they were walking along and talking together, suddenly a chariot of fire and horses of fire appeared and separated the two of them, and Elijah went up to heaven in a whirlwind. Elisha saw this and cried out...
Elisha	My father! My father! The chariots and horsemen of Israel!
Narrator	And Elisha saw him no more. Then he took hold of his garment and tore it in two. Elisha then picked up Elijah's cloak that had fallen from him and went back and stood on the bank of the Jordan. He took the cloak that had fallen from Elijah and struck the water with it.
Elisha	Where now is the LORD, the God of Elijah?
Narrator	When he struck the water, it divided to the right and to the left, and he crossed over. The company of the prophets from Jericho, who were watching, said...
Company	The spirit of Elijah is resting on Elisha.
Narrator	And they went to meet him and bowed to the ground before him.
Company	Look, we your servants have fifty able men. Let them go and look for your master. Perhaps the Spirit of the LORD has picked him up and set him down on some mountain or in some valley.
Elisha	No, do not send them.
Narrator	But they persisted until he was too embarrassed to refuse. So he said...

Elisha   Send them.

Narrator   And they sent fifty men who searched for three days but did not find him. When they returned to Elisha, who was staying in Jericho, he said to them...

Elisha   Didn't I tell you not to go?

Daniel's Training in Babylon

Daniel 1: 1-20 (ESV)

You will need:

Actors   Props

    Narrator   Water

    Daniel   Vegetables

    Ashpenaz (Eunuch)   Royal food

    Steward (non-speaking)   Wine (juice)

    Shadrach (non-speaking)   Table

    Meshach (non-speaking)

    Abednego (non-speaking)

    Guard (non-speaking)

Tips:

- This story is mostly narration. Have the students act out the scene while the narrator reads.
- Royal food can be anything other than vegetables. Place the royal food and juice on the table and let the steward swap it out with vegetables and water during the scene.

Set the scene:

Nebuchadnezzar was king of Babylon. The same year he became king, he surrounded Jerusalem and took many men and women back to Babylon as captives.

Discussion ideas:

- Daniel and his friends made a decision to be faithful to the laws of God. The Bible says that Daniel "resolved not to defile himself." Resolve is a strong word that means to be devoted to a principle or committed to a course of action.

When the temptation came, they did not hesitate because they had already resolved to be faithful. We sometimes find ourselves pressured to compromise our standards and live like the world around us. Merely wanting God's will is not enough to help us stand against this temptation. We must resolve to obey God.

- Do you think it would have been easier for Daniel and his friends to just eat what the king gave them? It took courage for them to stand up for what they believed. Can you think of a time when you were tempted to fit in rather than obey God? How did you handle it?

Narrator   In the third year of the reign of Jehoiakim king of Judah, Nebuchadnezzar king of Babylon came to Jerusalem and besieged it. And the Lord gave Jehoiakim king of Judah into his hand, with some of the vessels of the house of God. And he brought them to the land of Shinar, to the house of his god, and placed the vessels in the treasury of his god. Then the king commanded Ashpenaz, his chief eunuch, to bring some of the people of Israel, both of the royal family and of the nobility, youths without blemish, of good appearance and skillful in all wisdom, endowed with knowledge, understanding learning, and competent to stand in the king's palace, and to teach them the literature and language of the Chaldeans. The king assigned them a daily portion of the food that the king ate, and of the wine that he drank. They were to be educated for three years, and at the end of that time they were to stand before the king. Among these were Daniel, Hananiah, Mishael, and Azariah of the tribe of Judah. And the chief of the eunuchs gave them names: Daniel he called Belteshazzar, Hananiah he called Shadrach, Mishael he called Meshach, and Azariah he called Abednego. But Daniel resolved that he would not defile himself with the king's food, or with the wine that he drank. Therefore he asked the chief of the eunuchs to allow him not to defile himself. Then God gave Daniel favor and compassion in the sight of the chief of the Eunuchs, and the chief of the eunuchs said to Daniel...

Ashpenaz   I fear my lord the king, who assigned your food and your drink; for why should he see that you were in worse condition than the youths who are of your own age? So you would endanger my head with the king.

Daniel   Test your servants for ten days; let us be given vegetables to eat and water to drink. Then let our appearance and the appearance of the youths who eat the king's food be observed by you, and deal with your servants according to what you see.

Narrator   So he listened to them in this matter, and tested them for ten days. At the end of ten days it was seen that they were better in appearance and fatter in flesh than all the youths who ate the king's food. So the steward took away their food and the wine they were to drink, and gave them vegetables. As for these four youths, God gave them learning and skill in all literature and wisdom, and Daniel had understanding in all visions and dreams. At the end of the time, when the king had commanded that they should be brought in, the chief of the eunuchs brought them in before Nebuchadnezzar. And the king spoke with them, and among all of them none was found like Daniel, Hananiah, Mishael, and Azariah. Therefore they stood before the king. And in every matter of wisdom and understanding about which the king inquired of them, he found them ten times better than all the magicians and enchanters that were in all his kingdom.

The Image of Gold and the Fiery Furnace

Daniel 3 (ESV)

You will need:

Actors

    Narrator

    King Nebuchadnezzar

    Counselor

    Herald

    Chaldean

    Shadrach

    Meshach (non-speaking)

    Abednego (non-speaking)

    4th Person (non-speaking)

    King's men (non-speaking)

Props

    Statue

    Furnace

    Horn

    Rope

Tips:

- Use a podium or similar tall object covered with a sheet to create a statue.
- Place chairs in a circle to create a furnace that the actors can "go into".
- Have a fourth person already in the furnace, perhaps hidden under a sheet, until the others are thrown into the fire.

Set the scene:

Nebuchadnezzar was king of Babylon. Daniel, Shadrach, Meshach, and Abednego were brought to King Nebuchadnezzar to be trained to be leaders of his palace. Daniel was appointed a high position and made ruler over the entire province of Babylon. At Daniel's request, Shadrach, Meshach and Abednego were appointed as administrators over the province of Babylon.

Discussion Ideas:

- There are several excuses the men could have given to justify bowing to the image and saving their lives. They could have said they would "bow" but not "worship" or that they had to because they owed it to the king. But, worshiping the idol would violate God's command and damage their testimony to God. Can you think of a time when you made excuses to justify doing something wrong?

- They made a choice to obey God even though it could have cost them their lives. But, God proved faithful and saved them in a miraculous way. Can this story help you make a decision to obey God when you are faced with temptation? How?

Narrator King Nebuchadnezzar made an image of gold, whose height was sixty cubits and its breadth six cubits. He set it up on the plain of Dura, in the province of Babylon. Then King Nebuchadnezzar sent to gather the satraps, the prefects, and the governors, the counselors, the treasurers, the justices, the magistrates, and all the officials of the provinces to come to the dedication of the image that King Nebuchadnezzar had set up. Then the satraps, the prefects, and the governors, the counselors, the treasurers, the justices, the magistrates, and all the officials of the provinces gathered for the dedication of the image that King Nebuchadnezzar had set up. And they stood before the image that Nebuchadnezzar had set up. And the herald proclaimed aloud...

Herald You are commanded, O peoples, nations, and languages, that when you hear the sound of the horn, pipe, lyre, trigon, harp, bagpipe, and every kind of music, you are to fall down and worship the golden image that King Nebuchadnezzar has set up. And whoever does not fall down and worship shall immediately be cast into a burning fiery furnace. Therefore, as soon as all the peoples heard the sound of the horn, pipe, lyre, trigon, harp, bagpipe, and every kind of music, all the peoples, nations, and languages fell down and worshiped the golden image that King Nebuchadnezzar had set up. Therefore at the time certain Chaldeans came forward and maliciously accused the Jews. They declared to King Nebuchadnezzar...

Chaldean O king, live forever! You, O king, have made a decree, that every man who hears the sound of the horn, pipe, lyre, trigon, harp, bagpipe, and every kind of music, shall fall down and worship the golden image. And whoever does not fall down and worship shall be cast into a burning fiery furnace. There are certain Jews who you have appointed over the affairs of the province of Babylon: Shadrach, Meshach, and Abednego. These men, O king, pay no attention to you; they do not serve your gods or worship the golden image that you have set up.

Narrator Then Nebuchadnezzar in furious rage commanded that Shadrach, Meshach, and Abednego be brought. So they brought these men before the king.

King Is it true, O Shadrach, Meshach, and Abednego, that you do not serve my gods or worship the golden image that I have set up? Now if you are ready when you hear the sound of the horn, pipe, lyre, trigon, harp, bagpipe, and every kind of music, to fall down and worship the image that I have made, well and good. But if you do not worship, you shall   immediately be cast into a burning fiery furnace. And who is the god who will deliver you out of my hands?

Shadrach   O Nebuchadnezzar, we have no need to answer you in this matter. If this be so, Our God whom we serve is able to deliver us from the burning fiery furnace, and he will deliver us out of your hand, O king. But if not, be it known to you, O king, that we will not serve your gods or worship the golden image that you have set up.

Narrator   Then Nebuchadnezzar was filled with fury, and the expression of his face was changed against Shadrach, Meshach, and Abednego. He ordered the furnace heated seven times more than it was usually heated. And he ordered some of the mighty men of his army to bind Shadrach, Meshach, and Abednego, and to cast them into the burning fiery furnace. Then these men were bound in their cloaks, their tunics, their hats, and their other garments, and they were thrown into the burning fiery furnace. Because the king's order was urgent and the furnace overheated, the flame of the fire killed those men who took up Shadrach, Meshach, and Abednego. And these three men, Shadrach, Meshach, and Abednego, fell bound into the burning fiery furnace. Then King Nebuchadnezzar was astonished and rose up in haste. He declared to his counselors...

King   Did we not cast three men bound into the fire?

Counselor   True, O king.

King   But I see four men unbound, walking in the midst of the fire, and they are not hurt; and the appearance of the fourth is like a son of the gods.

Narrator   Then Nebuchadnezzar came to the door of the burning fiery furnace; he declared...

King   Shadrach, Meshach, and Abednego, servants of the Most High God, come out, and come here!

Narrator   Then Shadrach, Meshach, and Abednego came out from the fire. And the satraps, the prefects, the governors, and the king's counselor gathered together and saw that the fire had not had any power over the bodies of those men. The hair of their heads was not singed, their cloaks were not harmed, and no smell of fire had come upon them.

King   Blessed be the God of Shadrach, Meshach, and Abednego, who has sent his angel and delivered his servants, who trusted in him, and set aside the king's command, and yielded up their bodies rather than serve and worship any god except their own God. Therefore I make a decree: Any people, nation, or language that speaks anything against the God of Shadrach, Meshach, and Abednego shall be torn limb from limb, and their houses laid in ruins, for there is no other god who is able to rescue in this way.

Narrator   Then the king promoted Shadrach, Meshach, and Abednego in the province of Babylon.

The Handwriting on the Wall

Daniel 5 (ESV)

You will need:

Actors   Props

      Narrator   Regular cups

      King Belshazzar   Gold/Silver goblets (fancy cups)

      Queen   Purple robe

      Daniel   Gold chain

      Enchanter (non-speaking)   Words:

      Astrologer (non-speaking)   MEME, MEME

      Chaldeans (non-speaking)   TEKEL

                                        PARSIN

Tips:

- Explain to the students what an enchanter, astrologer and Chaldean are.

    o   Enchanter – a sorcerer, a controller of evil spirits
    o   Astrologer - influences the stars and planets
    o   Chaldeans – the Chaldeans were known for their knowledge of astrology

- Have the words written on pieces of paper and have a student tape them to the wall at the appropriate time during the drama.

Set the scene:

Sixty-six years has passed since King Nebuchadnezzar waged war against Jerusalem where he took articles, including gold goblets, from the temple of God. King Nebuchadnezzar has been driven out of town and King Belshazzar is now king.

Discussion ideas:

- Belshazzar used the goblets from the temple for his party and God condemned him for this act. We must not use what is set apart for God for our own purposes. Can you think of ways people might misuse things today? What about church buildings and financial donations?
- Belshazzar knew about God, but purposefully defied him. Because of this, he lost his kingdom and his life. How can we keep from purposefully sinning against God? We can make time for prayer and reading God's word every day. We can ask God to keep our hearts and mind pure. When we do sin (we all sin), we can ask God to forgive us.

Narrator   King Belshazzar made a great feast for a thousand of his lords and drank wine in front of the thousand. Belshazzar, when he tasted the wine, commanded that the vessels of gold and of silver that Nebuchadnezzar his father had taken out of the temple in Jerusalem be brought, that the king and his lords, his wives, and his concubines might drink from them. Then they brought in the golden vessels that had been taken out of the temple, the house of God in Jerusalem, and the king and his lords, his wives, and his concubines drank from them. They drank wine and praised the gods of gold and silver, bronze, iron, wood, and stone. Immediately the fingers of a human hand appeared and wrote on the plaster of the wall of the king's palace, opposite the lampstand. And the king saw the hand as it wrote. Then the king's color changed, and his thoughts alarmed him; his limbs gave way, and his knees knocked together. The king called loudly to bring in the enchanters, the Chaldeans, and the astrologers. The king declared to the wise men of Babylon...

King   Whoever reads this writing, and shows me its interpretation, shall be clothed with purple and have a chain of gold around his neck and shall be the third ruler in the kingdom.

Narrator   Then all the king's wise men came in, but they could not read the writing or make known to the king the interpretation. Then King Belshazzar was greatly alarmed, and his color changed, and his lords were perplexed. The queen, because of the words of the king and his lords, came into the banqueting hall, and the queen declared...

Queen   O king, live forever! Let not your thoughts alarm you or your color change. There is a man in your kingdom in whom is the spirit of the holy gods. In the days of your father, light and understanding and wisdom like the wisdom of the gods were found in him, and King Nebuchadnezzar, your father—your father the king—made him chief of the magicians, enchanters, Chaldeans, the Astrologers, because an excellent spirit, knowledge, and understanding to interpret dreams, explain riddles, and solve problems were found in this Daniel, whom the king named Belteshazzar. Now let Daniel be called, and he will show the interpretation.

Narrator   Then Daniel was brought in before the king. The king answered and said to Daniel...

King   You are that Daniel, one of the exiles of Judah, whom the king my father brought from Judah. I have heard of you that the spirit of the gods is in you, and that light and understanding and excellent wisdom are found in you. Now the wise men, the enchanters, have been brought in before me to read this writing and make known to me its interpretation, but they could not show the interpretation of the matter. But I have heard that you can give interpretations and solve problems. Now if you can read the writing and make known to me its interpretation, you shall be clothed with purple and have a chain of gold around your neck and shall be the third ruler in the kingdom.

Narrator   Then Daniel answered and said before the king...

Daniel   Let your gifts be for yourself, and give your rewards to another. Nevertheless, I will read the writing to the king and make known to him the interpretation. O king, the Most High God gave Nebuchadnezzar your father kingship and greatness and glory and majesty. And because of the greatness that he gave him, all people, nations, and languages trembled and feared before him. Whom he would, he killed, and whom he would, he kept alive; whom he would, he raised up, and whom he would, he humbled. But when his heart was lifted up and his spirit was hardened so that he dealt proudly, he was brought down from his kingly throne, and his glory was taken from him. He was driven from among the children of mankind, and his mind was made like that of a beast, and his dwelling was with the wild donkeys. He was fed grass like an ox, and his body was wet with the dew of heaven, until he knew that the Most High God rules the kingdom of mankind and sets over it whom he will. And you his son, Belshazzar, have not humbled you heart, though you knew all this, but you have lifted up yourself against the Lord of heaven. And the vessels of his house have been brought in before you and you and your lords, your wives, and your concubines have drunk wine from them. And you have praised the gods of silver and gold, of bronze, iron, wood, and stone, which do not see or hear or know, but the God in whose hand is your breath, and whose are all you ways, you have not honored. Then from his presence the hand was sent, and writing was inscribed. And this is the writing that was inscribed: Mene, Mene, Tekel, and

Parsin. This is the interpretation of the matter; Mene, God has numbered the days of your kingdom and brought it to an end; Tekel, you have been weighed in the balances and found wanting; Peres, your kingdom is divided and given to the Medes and Persians.

Narrator   Then Belshazzar gave the command, and Daniel was clothed with purple, a chain or gold was put around his neck, and proclamation was made about him, that he should be the third ruler in the kingdom. That very night Belshazzar the Chaldean king was killed. And Darius the Mede received the kingdom, being about sixty-two years old.

Daniel and the Lions' Den

Daniel 6: 1-27 (ESV)

You will need:

Actors   Props
    Narrator   Lions
    Men (one speaking)   Stone to cover den
    Satraps
    Daniel
    King Darius

Tips:

- Put stuffed animals under a table for a lion's den.
- Create a stone from cardboard.

Set the Scene:

Daniel did everything that was expected of him and the king respected him for it. The other rulers were jealous and wanted to do away with him.

Discussion ideas:

- Daniel was faithful to God over and over, even when it could have cost him a great sacrifice. Because of his faithfulness, the king and other officials became convinced of God's power. We need to be faithful to God all the time so God can use us to make an impact on others. If we are only faithful some of the time, what testimony do we give? What kind of testimony do you give with your daily life? Do others find you faithful?
- The people who were working for the king were jealous of Daniel because of his position with the king. Have you ever been in a position where your friends, classmates, or siblings were jealous of you? What happened? Have you ever been jealous of someone else? How did you deal with it?

Narrator   It pleased Darius to set over the kingdom 120 satraps, to be throughout the whole kingdom; and over them three high officials, of whom Daniel was one, to whom these satraps should give account, so that the king might suffer no loss. Then this Daniel became distinguished above all the other high officials and satraps, because an excellent spirit was in him. And the king planned to set him over the whole kingdom. Then the high officials and the satraps sought to find a ground for complaint against Daniel with regard to the kingdom, but they could find no ground for complaint or any fault, because he was faithful, and no error or fault was found in him. Then these men said...

Men   We shall not find any ground for complaint against this Daniel unless we find it in connection with the law of his God.

Narrator   Then these high officials and satraps came by agreement to the king and said to him...

Satraps   O King Darius, live forever! All the high officials of the kingdom, the perfects and the satraps, the counselors and the governors are agreed that the king should establish an ordinance and enforce an injunction, that whoever makes petition to any god or man for thirty days, except to you, O king, shall be cast into the den of lions. Now, O king, establish the injunction and sign the document, so that it cannot be changed, according to the law of the Medes and the Persians, which cannot be revoked.

Narrator   Therefore King Darius signed the document and injunction. When Daniel knew that the document had been signed, he went to his house where he had windows in his upper chamber open toward Jerusalem. He got down on his knees three times a day and prayed and gave thanks before his God, as he had done previously. Then these men came by agreement and found Daniel making petition and plea before his God. Then they came near and said before the king, concerning the injunction...

Satraps   O king! Did you not sign an injunction, that anyone who makes petition to any god, or man within thirty days except to you, O king, shall be cast into the den of Lions?

King	The thing stands fast, according to the law of the Medes and Persians, which cannot be revoked.
Satraps	Daniel, who is one of the exiles from Judah, pays no attention to you, O king, or the injunction you have signed, but makes his petition three times a day.
Narrator	Then the king, when he heard these words, was much distressed and set his mind to deliver Daniel. And he labored till the sun went down to rescue him. Then these men came by agreement to the king and said to the king...
Satraps	Know, O king, that it is a law of the Medes and Persians that no injunction or ordinance that the king establishes can be changed.
Narrator	Then the king commanded, and Daniel was brought and cast into the den of lions. The king declared to Daniel...
King	May your God, whom you serve continually, deliver you!
Narrator	And a stone was brought and laid on the mouth of the den, and the king sealed it with his own signet and with the signet of his lords, that nothing might be changed concerning Daniel. Then the king went to his palace and spent the night fasting; no diversions were brought to him, and sleep fled from him. Then, at break of day, the king arose and went in haste to the den of lions. As he came near to the den where Daniel was, he cried out in a tone of anguish. The king declared to Daniel...
King	O Daniel, servant of the living God, has your God, whom you serve continually, been able to deliver you from the lions?
Daniel	O king, live forever! My God sent his angel and shut the lions' mouths, and they have not harmed me, because I was found blameless before him; and also before you, O king, I have done no harm.
Narrator	Then the king was exceedingly glad, and commanded that Daniel be taken up out of the den. So Daniel was taken up out of the den, and no kind of harm was found on him, because he had trusted in his God. And the king commanded,

and those men who had maliciously accused Daniel were brought and cast into the den of lions—they, their children, and their wives. And before they reached the bottom of the den, the lions overpowered them and broke all their bones in pieces. Then King Darius wrote to all the peoples, nations, and languages that dwell in all the earth:

King   Peace be multiplied to you. I make a decree, that in all my royal dominion people are to tremble and fear before the God of Daniel, for he is the living God, enduring forever; his kingdom shall never be destroyed, and his dominion shall be to the end. He delivers and rescues; he works signs and wonders in heaven and on earth, he who has saved Daniel from the power of the lions.

Jonah Flees From the Lord

Jonah 1-3 (ESV)

You will need:

Actors	Props
Narrator	Boat
Lord	Big fish
Captain	Sackcloth
Sailor	Stones to cast lots
Jonah	Cargo (see tips)

Tips:

- Turn a table upside down and cover with a sheet and possibly fishing net to create a boat.
- Cover another table with a sheet to make a big fish.
- Designate a location for Nineveh.
- Sackcloth is rough clothing worn as a sign for repentance. Use pieces of scrap material or construction paper.
- Have cargo available for the sailors to throw overboard: empty boxes or pillows.

Set the scene:

Nineveh was the most important city in Assyria and would soon become the capital of the huge Assyrian empire. However, Nineveh was also a very wicked city.

Discussion ideas:

- Jonah didn't want to go to Nineveh, so he tried to run from God. He soon realized that no matter where he went, he couldn't get away from God. Have you ever felt God asking you to do something that you didn't want to do? Did you want to run from God? How did you handle it?

- The people of Nineveh had turned away from God. God could have just destroyed them, but He showed his love for all people and sent Jonah to give them God's message. Because Jonah obeyed (finally), the people of Nineveh repented and turned from their evil ways. Great things happen when we obey God's instructions. Have you ever felt God calling you to do something? What happened?

Narrator	Now the word of the Lord came to Jonah the son of Amittai, saying...
Lord	Arise, go to Nineveh, that great city, and call out against it, for their evil has come up before me.
Narrator	But Jonah rose to flee to Tarshish from the presence of the Lord. He went down to Joppa and found a ship going to Tarshish. So he paid the fare and went down into it, to go with them to Tarshish, away from the presence of the Lord. But the Lord hurled a great wind upon the sea, and there was a mighty tempest on the sea, so that the ship threatened to break up. Then the mariners were afraid, and each cried out to his god. And they hurled the cargo that was in the ship into the sea to lighten it for them. But Jonah had gone down into the inner part of the ship and had lain down and was fast asleep. So the captain came and said to him...
Captain	What do you mean, you sleeper? Arise, call out to your god! Perhaps the god will give a thought to us, that we may not perish. And they said to one another...
Sailor	Come, let us cast lots, that we may know on whose account this evil has come upon us.
Narrator	So they cast lots, and the lot fell on Jonah. Then they said to him...
Sailor	Tell us on whose account this evil has come upon us. What is your occupation? And where do you come from? What is your country? And of what people are you?
Jonah	I am a Hebrew, and I fear the Lord, the God of heaven, who made the sea and the dry land.
Narrator	Then the men were exceedingly afraid and said to him...
Sailor	What is this that you have done!
Narrator	For the men knew that he was fleeing from the presence of the Lord, because he had told them. Then they said to him...

Sailor	What shall we do to you, that the sea may quiet down or us?
Narrator	For the sea grew more and more tempestuous. He said to them...
Jonah	Pick me up and hurl me into the sea; then the sea will quiet down for you, for I know it is because of me that this great tempest has come upon you.
Narrator	Nevertheless, the men rowed hard to get back to dry land, but they could not, for the sea grew more and more tempestuous against them. Therefore they called out to the Lord...
Sailor	O Lord, let us not perish for this man's life, and lay not on us innocent blood, for you, O Lord, have done as it pleased you.
Narrator	So they picked up Jonah and hurled him into the sea, and the sea ceased from its raging. Then the men feared the Lord exceedingly, and they offered a sacrifice to the Lord and made vows. And the Lord appointed a great fish to swallow up Jonah. And Jonah was in the belly of the fish three days and three nights. Then Jonah prayed to the Lord his God from the belly of the fish, saying...
Jonah	I called out to the Lord, out of my distress, and he answered me; out of the belly of Sheol I cried, and you heard my voice. For you cast me into the deep, into the heart of the seas and the flood surrounded me; all your waves and your billows passed over me. Then I said, 'I am driven away from your sight; yet I shall again look upon your holy temple.' The waters closed in over me to take my life; the deep surrounded me; weeds were wrapped about my head at the roots of the mountains. I went down to the land whose bars closed upon me forever; yet you brought up my life from the pit, O Lord my God. When my life was fainting away, I remembered the Lord, and my prayer came to you, into your holy temple. Those who pay regard to vain idols forsake their hope of steadfast love. But I with the voice of thanksgiving will sacrifice to you; what I have vowed I will pay. Salvation belongs to the Lord!
Narrator	And the Lord spoke to the fish, and it vomited Jonah out upon the dry land. Then the word of the Lord came to Jonah the second time, saying...

Lord   Arise, go to Nineveh, that great city, and call out against it the message that I tell you.

Narrator   So Jonah arose and went to Nineveh, according to the word of the Lord. Now Nineveh as an exceedingly great city, three days journey in breadth. Jonah began to go into the city, going a day's journey. And he called out...

Jonah   Yet forty days, and Nineveh shall be overthrown!

Narrator   And the people of Nineveh believed God. They called for a fast and put on sackcloth, from the greatest of them to the least of them. The word reached the king of Nineveh, and he arose from his throne, removed his robe, covered himself with sackcloth, and sat in ashes. And he issued a proclamation and published through Nineveh...

Jonah   By the decree of the king and his nobles: Let neighbor man nor beast, herd nor flock, taste anything. Let them not feed or drink water, but let man and beast be covered with sackcloth, and let them call out mightily to God. Let everyone turn from his evil way and from the violence that is in his hands. Who knows? God may turn and relent and turn from his fierce anger, so that we may not perish.

Narrator   When God saw what they did, how they turned from their evil way, God relented of the disaster that he had said he would do to them, and he did not do it.

NEW TESTAMENT

John the Baptist

Luke 1: 5-25, 57-80 (TLB)

You will need:

Actors   Props

    Narrator   Baby

    Elizabeth   Tablet

    Angel   Pen

    Zachariah   Altar of incense

    Neighbor

    People (non-speaking)

Tips:

- Designate and area for the temple and an area for the home of Zachariah and Elizabeth.
- In the temple, place a candle on a small table or podium for an altar of incense.

Set the scene:

Elizabeth and Zachariah had been married for many years but were never blessed with a child. By now, they were well past the age when it is possible to have a child. Zachariah was a priest and the priests took turns serving at the temple.

Discussion ideas:

- Zachariah couldn't believe that he and his wife could ever have a child at their old age. God gave them a promise and then fulfilled the promise in His perfect timing. Are you waiting for God to answer a request or fulfill a need in your life? Sometimes we have to be patient for God's perfect timing.

- Because Zachariah questioned the angel and showed disbelief, God made him unable to speak until after the baby was born. He got his speech back as soon as they named the baby, John. Can you imagine having great news to tell and not being able to speak? This story can remind us not to question God and His perfect timing, even when it seems impossible to us.

Narrator   My story begins with a Jewish priest, Zacharias, who lived when Herod was king of Judea. Zacharias was a member of the Abijah division of the Temple service corps. (His wife Elizabeth was, like himself, a member of the priest tribe of the Jews, a descendant of Aaron.) Zacharias and Elizabeth were godly folk, careful to obey all of God's laws in spirit as well as in letter. But they had no children, for Elizabeth was barren; and now they were both very old. One day as Zacharias was going about his work in the Temple-for his division was on duty that week-the honor fell to him by lot to enter the inner sanctuary and burn incense before the Lord. Meanwhile, a great crowd stood outside in the Temple court, praying as they always did during that part of the service when the incense was being burned. Zacharias was in the sanctuary when suddenly an angel appeared, standing to the right of the altar of incense! Zacharias was startled and terrified,

Angel   Don't be afraid, Zacharias! For I have come to tell you that God has heard your prayer, and you wife Elizabeth will bear you a son! And you are to name him John. You will both have great joy and gladness at his birth, and many will rejoice with you. For he will be one of the the Lord's great men. He must never touch wine or hard liquor-and he will be filled with the Holy Spirit, even from before his birth! And he will persuade many a Jew to turn to the Lord his God. He will be a man of rugged spirit and power like Elijah, the prophet of old; and he will precede the coming of the Messiah, preparing the people for his arrival. He will soften adult hearts to become like little children's, and will change disobedient minds to the wisdom of faith.

Zacharias   But this is impossible! I'm an old man now, and my wife is also well along in years.

Angel   I am Gabriel! I stand in the very presence of God. It was he who sent me to you with this good news! And now, because you haven't believed me, you are to be stricken silent, unable to speak until the child is born. For my words will certainly come true at the proper time.

Narrator   Meanwhile the crowds outside were waiting for Zacharias to appear and wondered why he was taking so long. When he finally came out, he couldn't speak to them, and they realized from his gestures that he must have seen a vision in the Temple. He stayed on at the Temple for the remaining days for his Temple duties and then returned home. Soon afterwards Elizabeth his wife became pregnant and went into seclusion for five months.

Elizabeth   How kind the Lord is, to take away my disgrace of having no children.

Narrator   By now Elizabeth's waiting was over, for the time had come for the baby to be born-and it was a boy. The word spread quickly to her neighbors and relatives of how kind the Lord had been to her and everyone rejoiced. When the baby was eight days old, all the relatives and friends came for the circumcision ceremony. They all assumed the baby's name would Zacharias, after his father.

Elizabeth   No! He must be named John!

Neighbor   What? There is no one in all your family by that name.

Narrator   So they asked the baby's father, talking to him by gestures. He motioned for a piece of paper and to everyone's surprise wrote.

Zacharias   [Write on a tablet] His name is John.

Narrator   Instantly Zacharias could speak again, and he began praising God. Wonder fell upon the whole neighborhood, and the news of what had happened spread through the Judean hills. And everyone who heard about it thought long thoughts and asked...

Neighbor   I wonder what this child will turn out to be? For the hand of the Lord is surely upon him in some special way.

Narrator   Then his father Zacharias was filled with the Holy Spirit and gave this prophecy...

Zacharias   Praise the Lord, the God of Israel, for he has come to visit his people and has redeemed them. He is sending us a Mighty Savior from the royal line of his servant David, just as he promised through his holy prophets long ago-someone to save us from our enemies, from all who hate us. He has been merciful to our ancestors, yes, to Abraham himself, by remembering his sacred promise to him, and by granting us the privilege of serving God fearlessly, freed from our enemies, and by making us holy and acceptable, ready to stand in his presence forever. And you, my little son, shall be called the prophet of the glorious God, for you will prepare the way for the Messiah. You will tell his people how to find salvation through forgiveness of their sins. All this will be because the mercy of our God is very tender, and heaven's dawn is about to break upon us, to give light to those who sit in darkness and death's shadow, and to guide us to the path of peace.

Narrator   The little boy greatly loved God and when he grew up he lived out in the lonely wilderness until he began his public ministry to Israel.

The Birth of Jesus Foretold

Luke 1: 25-56, Matthew 1: 19-25 (NKJ)

You will need:

Actors	Props
Narrator	Bed
Gabriel (the Angel)	
Mary	
Elizabeth	
Joseph	
Angel	

Tips:

- Designate an area for Mary's home in Nazareth, an area for Elizabeth's home in Judea, and an area for Joseph's home in Nazareth
- Put a sheet over a table for a bed in Joseph's house.

Set the scene:

Mary and Elizabeth were related. An angel had appeared to Zachariah, Elizabeth's husband, in their old age and told them they would have a child. Elizabeth is now six months pregnant. Mary and Joseph were betrothed (engaged), but not yet married.

Discussion ideas:

- Mary was just an ordinary person. Being young, poor and female would have made her seem, in her day, unlikely to be used by God. However, she was chosen for one of the greatest miracles of all- to become the mother of the Messiah. Do you ever feel like you are too young or don't have enough experience to be used by God? Don't worry about your abilities. God can use you if you just trust Him.

- Nothing is impossible with God. He caused Mary to conceive a child without a earthly father, something scientists will tell you is impossible. He has performed miracle after miracle and He still performs miracles today. Can you think of a time when God answered a prayer in a way that you thought was impossible?

- Do you think Mary was afraid? Do you think she worried about what people would think of her conceiving a child before she was married? Because of Mary's faithfulness, our Savior was born just as God had planned. God has a plan for all of us. Pray now that you will be faithful when God reveals His plans for your life.

Scene: Mary's House

Narrator   Now in the sixth month the angel Gabriel was sent by God to a city of Galilee named Nazareth, to a virgin betrothed to a man whose name was Joseph, of the house of David. The virgin's name was Mary. And having come in, the angel said to her...

Gabriel   Rejoice, highly favored one, the Lord is with you: blessed are you among women!

Narrator   But when she saw him, she was troubled at this saying, and considered what manner of greeting this was. Then the angel said to her...

Gabriel   Do not be afraid, Mary, for you have found favor with God. And behold, you will conceive in your womb and bring forth a Son, and shall call His name Jesus. He will be great, and will be called the Son of the Highest; and the Lord God will give Him the throne of His father David. And He will reign over the house of Jacob forever, and of His kingdom there will be no end.

Mary   How can this be, since I do not know a man?

Gabriel   The Holy Spirit will come upon you, and the power of the Highest will overshadow you; therefore, also, that Holy One who is to be born will be called the Son of God. Now indeed, Elizabeth your relative has also conceived a son in her old age; and this is now the sixth month for her who was called barren. For with God nothing will be impossible.

Mary   Behold the maidservant of the Lord! Let it be to me according to your word.

Scene: Moving to Elizabeth's House

Narrator   And the angel departed from her. Now Mary arose in those days and went into the hill country with haste, to a city of Judah, and entered the house of Zacharias and greeted Elizabeth. And it happened, when Elizabeth heard the greeting of Mary, that the babe leaped in her womb; and Elizabeth was filled with the Holy Spirit. Then she spoke out with a loud voice and said...

Elizabeth   Blessed are you among women, and blessed is the fruit of your womb! But why is this granted to me, that the mother of my Lord should come to me? For indeed, as soon as the voice of your greeting sounded in my ears, the babe leaped in my womb for joy. Blessed is she who believed, for there will be a fulfillment of those things which were told her form the Lord.

Mary   My soul magnifies the Lord, and my spirit has rejoiced in God my Savior. For He has regarded the lowly state of His maidservant; for behold, henceforth all generations will call me blessed. For He who is mighty has done great things for me, and holy is His name. And His mercy is on those who fear Him from generation to generation. He has shown strength with His arm; He has scattered the proud in the imagination of their hearts. He has put down the mighty from their thrones, and exalted the lowly. He has filled the hungry with good things, and the rich He has sent away empty. He has helped His servant Israel, in remembrance of His mercy, as He spoke to our fathers, to Abraham and to his seed forever.

Narrator   And Mary remained with her about three months, and returned to her house.

Scene: Joseph's house

Narrator   Then Joseph her husband, being a just man, and not wanting to make her a public example, was minded to put her away secretly. But while he thought about these things, behold, an angel of the Lord appeared to him in a dream, saying...

Angel   Joseph, son of David, do not be afraid to take to you Mary your wife, for that which is conceived in her is of the Holy Spirit. And she will bring forth a Son, and you shall call His name Jesus, for He will save His people from their sins.

Narrator   So all this was done that it might be fulfilled which was spoken by the Lord through the prophet saying. "Behold, the virgin shall be with child, and bear a Son, and they shall call His name Immanuel, which is translated, "God with us. Then Joseph, being aroused from sleep, did as the angel of the Lord commanded him and took to him his wife and did not know her till she had brought forth her firstborn Son. And he called His name Jesus.

The Birth of Jesus

Luke 2: 1-20, Matthew 2: 1-23 (NKJ)

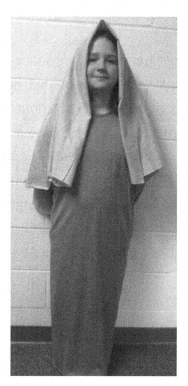

You will need:

Actors

        Narrator

        Angels (one speaking)

        Shepherds (one speaking)

        3 Wise men (one speaking)

        King Herod

        Mary (non-speaking)

        Joseph (non-speaking)

Props

        Stable

        Manger

        Baby doll (Jesus as a baby)

        Larger doll (Jesus as a toddler)

        Gifts (3)

        Star

Tips:

- Designate an area for the stable in Bethlehem, an area for Jerusalem, and an area for Mary and Joseph's house (also in Bethlehem).

- Turn a table on its side to create a stable.
- Use a basket or even a box with straw to create a manger.
- Jesus is one or two years old by the time the wise men visit him. Use a larger doll if you have one.
- Dim the lights between scenes to designate the passing of time.

Set the scene:

Mary and Joseph had both heard from an angel that Mary would give birth to a son and she became pregnant with a child.

Discussion ideas:

- God called Mary and Joseph to become the parents of Jesus, and it was not an easy task for them. They had to travel when she was pregnant. There were no rooms for them in Bethlehem, so they had to have the baby in a stable. They had to leave town to escape King Herod. Have you ever been asked to do something that turned out to be harder than you thought it would be? Remember that doing God's will doesn't necessarily mean a comfortable life. Sometimes we are asked to do things that are hard and uncomfortable.
- The wise men brought gifts to honor and worship Jesus. What can we do to honor and worship him today? Can we worship Him with our time and service as well as our money?

Scene: Moving from Nazareth to Bethlehem

Narrator And it came to pass in those days that a decree went out from Caesar Augustus that all the world should be registered. The census first took place while Quirinius was governing Syria. So all went to be registered, everyone to his own city. Joseph also went up from Galilee, out of the city of Nazareth, into Judea, to the city of David, which is called Bethlehem, because he was of the house and lineage of David, to be registered with Mary, his betrothed wife, who was with child. So it was, that while they were there, the days were completed for her to be delivered. And she brought forth her firstborn Son, and wrapped Him in swaddling cloths, and laid Him in a manger, because there was no room for them in the inn. Now there were in the same country shepherds living out in the fields, keeping watch over their flock by night. And behold, an angel of the Lord stood before them, and the glory of the Lord shone around them, and they were greatly afraid. Then the angel said to them...

Angel Do not be afraid, for behold, I bring you good tidings of great joy which will be to all people. For there is born to you this day in the city of David a Savior, who is Christ the Lord. And this will be the sign to you: You will find a Babe wrapped in swaddling cloths, lying in a manger.

Narrator And suddenly there was with the angel a multitude of the heavenly host praising God and saying...

Angel Glory to God in the highest, and on earth peace, goodwill toward men!

Narrator So it was, when the angels had gone away from them into heaven, that the shepherds said to one another...

Shepherd Let us now go to Bethlehem and see this thing that has come to pass, which the Lord has made known to us.

Narrator And they came with haste and found Mary and Joseph, and the Babe lying in a manger. Now when they had seen Him, they made widely known the saying which was told them concerning this Child. And all those who heard it marveled at those things which were told them by the shepherds. But Mary kept all these things and pondered them in her heart. Then the shepherds returned, glorifying and praising God for all the things that they had heard and seen, as it was told them.

Scene: Jerusalem

Narrator   In the days of Herod the king, behold, wise men from the East came to Jerusalem saying....

Wise men   [speaking to Herod] Where is He who has been born King of the Jews? For we have seen His star in the East and have come to worship Him.

Narrator   When Herod the king heard this, he was troubled, and all Jerusalem with him. And when he had gathered all the chief priests and scribes of the people together, he inquired of them where the Christ was to be born. So they said to him...

Wise men   In Bethlehem of Judea, for this it is written by the prophet: But you, Bethlehem, in the land of Judah, are not the least among the rulers of Judah; for out of you shall come a Ruler who will shepherd My people Israel.

Narrator   Then Herod, when he had secretly called the wise men, determined from them what time the star appeared. And he sent them to Bethlehem and said...

Herod   Go and search carefully for the young Child, and when you have found Him, bring back word to me, that I may come and worship Him also.

Scene: Moving from Jerusalem to Mary & Joseph's house in Bethlehem

Narrator   When they heard the king, they departed; and behold, the star which they had seen in the East went before them, till it came and stood over where the young Child was. When they saw the star, they rejoiced with exceedingly great joy. And when they had come into the house, they saw the young Child with Mary His mother, and fell down and worshiped Him. And when they had opened their treasures, they presented gifts to Him: gold, frankincense, and myrrh. Then, being divinely warned in a dream that they should not return to Herod, they departed for their own country another way.

Jesus at the Temple

Luke 2:39-52 (ESV)

You will need:

Actors   Props
    Narrator   Temple
    Mary
    Jesus
    Joseph (non-speaking)
    Teachers (non-speaking)
    Crowd of people (non-speaking)

Tips:

- Use chairs in a classroom arrangement to create a temple.
- Designate an area for the temple and a path to be the road between Nazareth and Jerusalem.

Set the scene:

The Feast of the Passover was observed by Jews every year to celebrate being delivered from Egypt. The Feast was held in Jerusalem. Jesus is now 12 years old and his family travelled from Nazareth, where they lived, to Jerusalem for the feast.

Discussion ideas:

- This passage ends by telling us that Jesus grew in wisdom and stature and in favor with God and men. The next account of Jesus in the Bible is when he is 30 years old. We don't know much about Jesus as a teenager, but we do know that He grew in wisdom, stature, and favor with God. Are you growing in these areas in your life? What kind of things can you do to accomplish this?

- At 12 years old, Jesus was in the temple listening to the teachers and asking them questions. What teachers has God put in your life that you can listen to and ask questions? Do you make it a priority to spend time with other believers to learn more about out Savior?

Narrator	And when they had performed everything according to the Law of the Lord, they returned into Galilee, to their own town of Nazareth. And the child grew and became strong, filled with wisdom. And the favor of God was upon him. Now his parents went to Jerusalem every year at the Feast of the Passover. And when he was twelve years old, they went up according to custom. And when the feast was ended, as they were returning, the boy Jesus stayed behind in Jerusalem. His parents did not know it, but supposing him to be in the group they went a day's journey, but then they began to search for him among their relatives and acquaintances, and when they did not find him, they returned to Jerusalem, searching for him. After three days they found him in the temple, sitting among the teachers, listening to them and asking them questions. And all who heard him were amazed at his understanding and his answers. And when his parents saw him, they were astonished. And his mother said to him...
Mary	Son, why have you treated us so? Behold, your father and I have been searching for you in great distress.
Jesus	Why were you looking for me? Did you not know that I must be in my Father's house?
Narrator	And they did not understand the saying that he spoke to them. And he went down with them and came to Nazareth and was submissive to them. And his mother treasured up all these things in her heart. And Jesus increased in wisdom and in statue and in favor with God and man.

The Baptism of Jesus

Matthew 3: 1-17 (ESV)

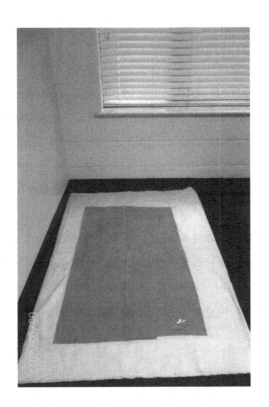

You will need:

Actors

    Narrator

    John

    Jesus

    Voice from Heaven

    People being baptized

      (non-speaking)

Props

    River

    Clothing for John

    Belt

Tips:

- Use a blue sheet to represent the Jordan River.
- Use a vest of fake fur for John's clothes, or be creative and use something you already have available to represent his odd clothing.

Set the scene:

> John the Baptist is at the Jordan River preaching and baptizing anyone who believes.

Discussion ideas:

- John felt unqualified to baptize Jesus and questioned his request. But Jesus explained that it would "fulfill all righteousness," which means to accomplish God's mission. Jesus, the perfect man, didn't need baptism, but accepted baptism in obedience to God. If you are a believer, have you been baptized? Being baptized allows us to publicly show that we have chosen to be obedient to God.

- The voice from heaven said, "This is my beloved son, with whom I am well pleased." Doesn't it feel good to hear your parents say they are pleased with you or proud of you? How much better will it feel to hear God say that about us? Are you living in a way that pleases God?

Narrator   In those days John the Baptist came preaching in the wilderness of Judea.

John   Repent, for the kingdom of heaven is at hand. For this is he who was spoken of by the prophet Isaiah when he said, "The voice of one crying in the wilderness: Prepare the way of the Lord; make his paths straight.

Narrator   Now John wore a garment of camel's hair and a leather belt around his waist, and his food was locusts and wild honey. Then Jerusalem and all Judea and all the region about the Jordan were going out to him, and they were baptized by him in the river Jordan, confessing their sins. But when he saw many of the Pharisees and Sadducces coming to his baptism, he said to them...

John   You brood of vipers! Who warned you to flee from the wrath to come? Bear fruit in keeping with repentance. And do not presume to say to yourselves, We have Abraham as our father, for I tell you, God is able from these stones to raise up children for Abraham. Even now the axe is laid to the root of the trees. Every tree therefore that does not bear good fruit is cut down and thrown into the fire. I baptize you with water for repentance, but he who is coming after me is mightier than I, whose sandals I am not worthy to carry. He will baptize you with the Holy Spirit and fire. His winnowing fork is in his hand, and he will clear his threshing floor and gather his wheat into the barn, but the chaff he will burn with unquenchable fire.

Narrator   Then Jesus came from Galilee to the Jordan to John, to be baptized by him. John would have prevented him saying...

John   I need to be baptized by you, and do you come to me?

Jesus   Let it be so now, for thus it is fitting for us to fulfill all righteousness.

Narrator   Then he consented. And when Jesus was baptized, immediately he went up from the water, and behold, the heavens were opened to him, and he saw the Spirit of God descending like a dove and coming to rest on him; and behold, a voice from heaven said..

Voice   This is my beloved Son, with whom I am well pleased.

Satan Tempts Jesus

Matthew 4: 1-11 (ESV)

You will need:

Actors   Props

    Narrator   Stones

    Jesus

    Devil

Tips:

- Use a brown/tan sheet to designate an area for the desert.
- Stage chairs to designate an area for the Holy City.
- Let the students stand on a table to designate the high mountain.

Set the scene:

Jesus has just been baptized by John the Baptist.

Discussion ideas:

- Jesus had been fasting for 40 days when He was tempted with food. The devil often chooses to tempt us when we are vulnerable or in our weakest time. Can you think of an example of a time when you might be susceptible to temptation? How can this scripture help you?
- Jesus Himself had to overcome temptation. He knows what we are experiencing when we are tempted and He can help us through the situation. When you are tempted, you can turn to Him for strength.
- Jesus used scriptures to resist the devil. In order to use scripture, we have to know scripture. Do you spend time learning and memorizing scripture? God's word is truly a gift, and we can use it to help us resist temptation.

| Narrator | Then Jesus was led by the Spirit into the wilderness to be tempted by the devil. And after fasting forty days and forty nights, he was hungry. And the tempter came and said to him... |

| Devil | If you are the Son of God, command these stones to become loaves of bread. |

| Jesus | It is written, man shall not live by bread alone, but by every word that comes from the mouth of God. |

| Narrator | Then the devil took him to the holy city and set him on the pinnacle of the temple and said to him... |

| Devil | If you are the Son of God, throw yourself down, for it is written. 'He will command his angels concerning you,' and 'On their hands they will bear you up, lest you strike your foot against a stone.' |

| Jesus | Again it is written, You shall not put the Lord your God to the test. |

| Narrator | Again, the devil took him to a very high mountain and showed him all the kingdoms of the world and their glory. And he said to him... |

| Devil | All these I will give you, if you will fall down and worship me. |

| Jesus | Be gone, Satan! For it is written, 'You shall worship the Lord your God and him only shall you serve.' |

| Narrator | Then the devil left him, and behold, angels came and were ministering to him. |

Jesus Is Rejected in Nazareth

Luke 4: 14-30 (ESV)

You will need:

Actors   Props
    Narrator   Scroll
    Jesus
    People

Tips:

- Attach cloth to two dowel rods to create a scroll. Print the scriptures and tape it to the cloth.

Set the scene:

John the Baptist has been arrested, so Jesus left Judea to return home to Nazareth.

Discussion ideas:

- Even in his hometown, Jesus was not accepted as a prophet. Your Christian lifestyles and faith may not be easily understood even among your family and friends. Don't be discouraged, this happened to Jesus too. Has a similar rejection happened to you or to someone you know?

Narrator   And Jesus returned in the power of the Spirit to Galilee, and a report about him went out through all the surrounding country. And he taught in their synagogues, being glorified by all. And he came to Nazareth, where he had been brought up. And as was his custom, he went to the synagogue on the Sabbath day, and he stood up to read. And the scroll of the prophet Isaiah was given to him. He unrolled the scroll and found the place where it was written.

Jesus   The Spirit of the Lord is upon me, because he has anointed me to proclaim good news to the poor. He has sent me to proclaim liberty to the captives and recovering of sight to the blind, to set at liberty those who are oppressed, to proclaim the year of the Lord's favor.

Narrator   And he rolled up the scroll and gave it back to the attendant and sat down. And the eyes of all in the synagogue were fixed on him. And he began to say to them...

Jesus   Today this Scripture has been fulfilled in your hearing.

Narrator   And all spoke well of him and marveled at the gracious words that were coming from his mouth. And they said...

People   Is not this Joseph's son?

Jesus   Doubtless you will quote to me this proverb, 'Physician, heal yourself.' What we have heard you did at Capernaum, do here in your hometown as well. Truly, I say to you, no prophet is acceptable in his hometown. But in truth, I tell you, there were many widows in Israel in the days of Elijah, when the heavens were shut up three years and six months, and a great famine came over all the land, and Elijah was sent to none of them, but only to Zarephath, in the land of Sidon, to a woman who was a widow. And there were many lepers in Israel in the time of the prophet Elisha, and none of them was cleansed, but only Naaman the Syrian.

Narrator   When they heard these things, all in the synagogue were filled with wrath. And they rose up and drove him out of the town and brought him to the brow of the hill on which their town was built, so that they could throw him down the cliff. But passing through their midst, he want away.

The Disciples Follow Jesus

Luke 5: 1-11, John 1: 43-51 (ESV)

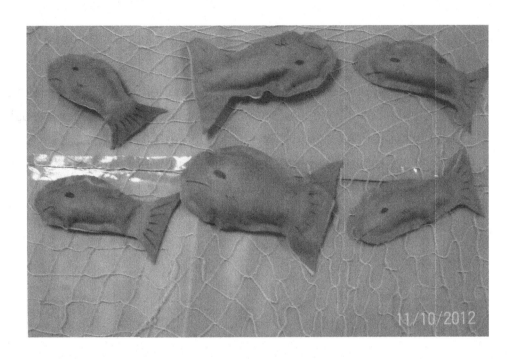

You will need:

Actors

    Narrator

    Jesus

    Simon

    Philip

    Nathanael

    Fishermen (non-speaking)

    James (non-speaking)

    John (non-speaking)

Props

    Boats (2)

    Fish

    Nets

Tips:

- Turn a table upside down and cover it with a sheet to create a boat.
- Purchase fishing net at the Dollar Store.
- Cut fish out of construction paper.

Set the scene:

> Jesus is preaching by the Lake of Gennesaret, which is also called the Sea of Galilee.

Discussion ideas:

- The fishermen pulled their boats to shore and left everything to follow him. Can you think of anyone who has left everything behind to follow Jesus? What about missionaries that serve in other countries?
- We may not be asked to leave everything, but we may be asked to sacrifice. Can you think of a time when you felt like you were called to give something up that you enjoyed in order to serve God? What happened?

Narrator   On one occasion, while the crowd was pressing in on him to hear the word of God, he was standing by the lake of Gennesaret, and he saw two boats by the lake, but the fishermen had gone out of them and were washing their nets. Getting into one of the boats, which was Simon's, he asked him to put out a little from the land. And he sat down and taught the people from the boat. And when he had finished speaking, he said to Simon...

Jesus   Put out into the deep and let down your nets for a catch. And Simon answered...

Simon   Master, we toiled all night and took nothing! But at your word I will let down the nets.

Narrator   And when they had done this, they enclosed a large number of fish, and their nets were breaking. They signaled to their partners in the other boat to come and help them. And they came and filled both the boats, so that they began to sink. But when Simon Peter saw it, he fell down at Jesus' knees, saying...

Peter   Depart from me, for I am a sinful man, O Lord.

Narrator   For he and all who were with him were astonished at the catch of fish that they had taken, and so also were James and John, sons of Zebedee, who were partners with Simon. And Jesus said to Simon...

Jesus   Do not be afraid; from now on you will be catching men.

Narrator   And when they had brought their boats to land, they left everything and followed him. The next day Jesus decided to go to Galilee. He found Philip and said to him...

Jesus   Follow me.

Narrator   Now Philip was from Bethsaida, the city of Andrew and Peter. Philip found Nathanael and said to him...

Philip   We have found him of whom Moses in the Law and also the prophets wrote, Jesus of Nazareth, the son of Joseph.

Nathanael   Can anything good come out of Nazareth?

Philip   Come and see.

Narrator   Jesus saw Nathanael coming toward him and said of him...

Jesus   Behold, an Israelite indeed, in whom there is no deceit!

Nathanael   How do you know me?

Jesus   Before Philip called you, when you were under the fig tree, I saw you.

Nathanael   Rabbi, you are the Son of God! You are the King of Israel!

Jesus   Because I said to you, 'I saw you under the fig tree,' do you believe? You will see greater things than these. Truly, truly, I say to you, you will see heaven opened, and the angels of God ascending and descending on the Son of Man.

Jesus Turns Water into Wine
John 2: 1-11 (ESV)

You will need:

Actors   Props

Narrator   Jars

Mary   Cups or glasses

Jesus   Water

Master of the Banquet   Powdered drink mix (optional)

Disciples (non-speaking)

Bride (non-speaking)

Groom (non-speaking)

Tips:

- Use a veil for the bride. The groom wore regular biblical costume clothing.
- Put powdered drink mix in the bottom of the jars to create a realistic scene of turning water into wine.

Set the scene:

Jesus and his disciples and his Mother are at a wedding.

Discussion ideas:

- Jesus turned ordinary water into the best tasting wine. Jesus has the ability to turn ordinary into extraordinary, and He can do that for our lives as well. If we put our trust in Jesus and seek His will for our lives, He can make our ordinary lives into something beautiful and extraordinary.

- Wedding ceremonies lasted for several days and the guests would eat and drink and celebrate with the bride and groom. Running out of wine would have been a big embarrassment for them. When Mary saw that there was a problem, she turned to Jesus, and we can do the same. When we have a problem, big or small, we can turn to Jesus as well.

- Jesus told the servants to fill the jars with water, and they obeyed. Because they obeyed, they were able to bring joy to others and got to witness a great miracle of Jesus. Have you ever been able to do something for others that brought them great joy and happiness? How did it make you feel? By serving others, we can allow God to use us to bring joy to others and we will be blessed with joy as well.

Narrator   On the third day there was a wedding at Cana in Galilee, and the mother of Jesus was there. Jesus also was invited to the wedding with his disciples. When the wine ran out, the mother of Jesus said to him...

Mary   They have no wine.

Jesus   Woman, what does this have to do with me? My hour as not yet come.

Narrator   His mother said to the servants...

Mary   Do whatever he tells you.

Narrator   Now there were six stone water jars there for the Jewish rites of purification, each holding twenty or thirty gallons. Jesus said to the servants...

Jesus   Fill the jars with water.

Narrator   And they filled them up to the brim. And he said to them...

Jesus   Now draw some out and take it to the master of the feast.

Narrator   So they took it. When the master of the feast tasted the water now become wine, and did not know where it came from (though the servants who had drawn the water knew), the master of the feast called the bridegroom and said to him...

Master   Everyone serves the good wine first, and when people have drunk freely, then the poor wine. But you have kept the good wine until now.

Narrator   This is the first of his signs, Jesus did at Cana in Galilee, and manifested his glory. And his disciples believed in him.

Jesus Teaches Nicodemus

John 3: 1-21 (ESV)

You will need:

Actors   Props

      Narrator

      Jesus

      Nicodemus

Tips:

- This scene takes place at night. Turn the lights off and use a flashlight.

Set the scene:

Nicodemus was one of the Pharisees, an influential group of Jews.

Discussion ideas:

- Nicodemus was a learned teacher himself, yet he came to Jesus to be taught. Even if we think we are smart and have all the answers, we need to come to Jesus with an open mind and allow him to show us His truth.
- Nicodemus was able to walk right up to Jesus and ask him a question. What are the ways that Jesus can teach us today?
- Jesus explained to Nicodemus that he had to be "born again." What do you think that means? Accepting God's gift of salvation gives us a new spiritual birth. We have already been born with a physical life. When we accept Christ as our Savior, the Holy Spirit comes into our lives and gives us a new spiritual birth.

Narrator   Now there was a man of the Pharisees named Nicodemus, a ruler of the Jews. This man came to Jesus by night and said to him...

Nicodemus   Rabbi, we know that you are a teacher come from God, for no one can do these signs that you do unless God is with him.

Jesus   Truly, truly, I say to you, unless one is born again he cannot see the kingdom of God.

Nicodemus   How can a man be born when he is old? Can he enter a second time into his mother's womb and be born?

Jesus   Truly, Truly, I say to you, unless one is born of water and the Spirit, he cannot enter the kingdom of God. That which is born of the flesh is flesh, and that which is born of the Spirit is spirit. Do not marvel that I said to you, 'You must be born again.' The wind blows where it wishes, and you hear its sound, but you do not know where it comes from or where it goes. So it is with everyone who is born of the Spirit.

Nicodemus   How can these things be?

Jesus   Are you the teacher of Israel and yet you do not understand these things? Truly, truly, I say to you, we speak of what we know, and bear witness to what we have seen, but you do not receive our testimony. If I have told you earthly things and you do not believe, how can you believe if I tell you heavenly things? No one has ascended into heaven except he who descended from heaven, the Son of Man. And as Moses lifted up the serpent in the wilderness, so must the Son of Man be lifted up, that whoever believes in him may have eternal life. For God so loved the world, that he gave his only Son, that whoever believes in him should not perish but have eternal life. For God did not send his Son into the world to condemn the world, but in order that the world might be saved through him. Whoever believes in him is not condemned, but whoever does not believe is condemned already, because he has not believed in the name of the only Son of God. And this is the judgment: the light has come into the world, and people loved the darkness rather than the light because their works were evil. For everyone who does wicked things hates the light and does not come to the light, lest his works should be exposed. But whoever does what is true comes to the light, so that it may be clearly seen that his works have been carried out in God.

Jesus Drives Out an Evil Spirit

Mark 1: 21-28 (ESV)

You will need:

Actors   Props

    Narrator

    Man

    People (one speaks)

    Jesus

Tips:

- Arrange chairs to set up a synagogue meeting or have students sit on the floor.

Set the scene:

Jesus has moved to Capernaum from Nazareth and is teaching in the synagogue.

Discussion ideas:

- The man was possessed by evil spirits. Evil spirits oppose God and work against people. However, evil spirits are powerless against God. What are ways we can guard ourselves against being influenced by evil spirits?
- Jesus was teaching at the synagogue and was interrupted by unclean spirits. Have you ever been in the middle of doing something good but got interrupted or sidetracked by something? Satan likes to interrupt our plans if we are doing something to further God's kingdom. We need to keep our focus on Christ and guard against distractions.
- What are some of the ways that Satan can interrupt or distract you from God's teachings? How can we guard against that happening?

Narrator   And they went into Capernaum, and immediately on the Sabbath he entered the synagogue and was teaching. And they were astonished at his teaching, for he taught them as one who had authority, and not as the scribes. And immediately there was in their synagogue a man with an unclean spirit. And he cried out...

Man   What have you to do with us, Jesus of Nazareth? Have you come to destroy us? I know who you are—the Holy One of God.

Narrator   But Jesus rebuked him, saying...

Jesus   Be silent, and come out of him!

Narrator   And the unclean spirit, convulsing him and crying out with a loud voice, came out of him. And they were all amazed, so that they questioned among themselves, saying...

People   What is this? A new teaching with authority! He commands even the unclean spirits, and they obey him.

Narrator   And at once his fame spread everywhere throughout all the surrounding region of Galilee.

Jesus Heals a Paralyzed Man

Mark 2: 1-12 (ESV)

You will need:

Actors   Props

    Narrator   Mat

    Jesus

    Scribes

    Four men to carry the

        mat (non-speaking)

    Paralytic (non-speaking)

Tips:

- Designate an area for the house and have everyone not playing a part crowd around so the four men cannot get into the house.
- Place a table adjacent to the house and let the actors use that for the roof.
- Use a beach towel for the mat. For safety, don't have the students actually carry the paralytic up on the roof on the mat – just pretend.

Set the scene:

Jesus has returned home to Capernaum and everyone wanted to hear him preach.

Discussion ideas:

- The friends of the paralyzed man had compassion on their friend and were moved to action to help him. When you see another person with a need, do you act?
- These four men knew that their friend needed Jesus and they did not give up. They could have just brought him to the house and said, "Good luck getting in," when they saw the crowd. But they didn't. Do you know anyone who doesn't yet know about Jesus? If so, look for opportunities to share Jesus with them and don't give up if the first attempt doesn't go well.

Narrator	And when he returned to Capernaum after some days, it was reported that he was at home. And many were gathered together, so that there was no more room, not even at the door. And he was preaching the word to them. And they came, bringing to him a paralytic carried by four men. And when they could not get near him because of the crowd, they removed the roof above him, and when they had made an opening, they let down the bed on which the paralytic lay. And when Jesus saw their faith, he said to the paralytic...
Jesus	Son, your sins are forgiven.
Narrator	Now some of the scribes were sitting there, questioning in their hearts.
Scribes	Why does this man speak like that? He is blaspheming! Who can forgive sins but God alone?
Narrator	And immediately Jesus, perceiving in his spirit that they thus questioned within themselves, said to them...
Jesus	Why do you question these things in your hearts? Which is easier, to say to the paralytic, 'your sins are forgiven,' or to say, 'Rise, take up your bed and walk?' But that you may know that the Son of Man has authority on earth to forgive sins—he said to the paralytic--- I say to you, rise, pick up your bed, and go home.
Narrator	And he rose and immediately picked up his bed and went out before them all, so that they were all amazed and glorified God, saying...
Scribes	We never saw anything like this!

Jesus Calms the Storm

Mark 4: 35-41 (ESV)

You will need:

Actors   Props

    Narrator   Boat

    Disciples (one speaks)   Cushion

    Jesus

Tips:

- Turn a table upside down and cover it with a sheet to create a boat. Add fishing net to make it look like a boat if you have it.
- Flash the lights to simulate a storm. Have students make waves with blue sheets and add sound effects for the wind and thunder.

Set the scene:

Jesus and his disciples are on a boat in the Sea of Galilee.

Discussion ideas:

- The disciples were afraid and beginning to panic. Have you ever been in a situation where you were beginning to panic? When this happens, we need to remember to trust God to care for us and seek His comfort.
- This is another one of Jesus's miracles. Even the wind and seas obeyed His voice. If He has the power to do that, He can surely help us through our tough situations. Just like the disciples called out to Him when they were scared, we can do the same.

| Narrator | On that day, when evening had come, he said to them... |

| Jesus | Let us go across to the other side. |

| Narrator | And leaving the crowd, they took him with them in the boat, just as he was. And other boats were with him. And a great windstorm arose, and the waves were breaking into the boat, so that the boat was already filling. But he was in their stern, asleep on the cushion. And they woke him and said to him... |

| Disciple | Teacher, do you not care that we are perishing? |

| Jesus | Peace! Be still! |

| Narrator | And the wind ceased, and there was a great calm. |

| Jesus | Why are you so afraid? Have you still no faith? |

| Narrator | And they were filled with great fear and said to one another... |

| Disciple | Who then is this, that even the wind and the sea obey him? |

Jesus Feeds Five Thousand

John 6: 1-15 (ESV)

You will need:

Actors	Props
Narrator	5 loaves of bread
Jesus	2 fish
Philip	Basket
Andrew	
Crowd (one speaking)	
Boy (non-speaking)	

Tips:

- Use a blue sheet to represent the Sea of Galilee.
- Use dinner rolls or hotdog buns for the loaves of bread. Cut fish out of construction paper.

Set the scene:

Jesus and the disciples were going away to be by themselves, but the crowd learned about it and followed him.

Discussion ideas:

- We sometimes limit God by determining what is and is not possible. Don't let your idea of impossible limit the way you let God use you. Have you ever felt like God was asking you to do something and you thought it was an impossible task? What did you do?
- Do you ever decide to do nothing because you think what you have to offer is not enough to make a difference? Don't worry about whether you have enough or not. God can take very little and use it in big ways. We need to be prepared to offer what we have and trust God to do the rest.

Scripture Alive in Your Classroom with Drama

Narrator	After this Jesus went away to the other side of the Sea of Galilee, which is the Sea of Tiberias. And a large crowd was following him, because they saw the signs that he was doing on the sick. Jesus went up on the mountain, and there he sat down with his disciples. Now the Passover, the feast of the Jews, was at hand. Lifting up his eyes, then, and seeing that a large crowd was coming toward him, Jesus said to Philip...
Jesus	Where are we to buy bread, so that these people may eat?
Narrator	He said this to test him, for he himself knew what he would do.
Philip	Two hundred denarii worth of bread would not be enough for each of them to get a little.
Narrator	One of his disciples, Andrew, Simon Peter's brother said to him...
Andrew	There is boy here who has five barley loaves and two fish, but what are they for so many?
Jesus	Have the people sit down.
Narrator	Now there was much grass in the place. So the men sat down, about five thousand in number. Jesus then took the loaves, and when he had given thanks, he distributed them to those who were seated. So also the fish, as much as they wanted. And when they had eaten their fill, he told his disciples...
Jesus	Gather up the leftover fragments, that nothing may be lost.
Narrator	So they gathered them up and filled twelve baskets with fragments from the five barley loaves left by those who had eaten. When the people saw the sign that he had done, they said...
Crowd	This is indeed the Prophet who is to come into the world!
Narrator	Perceiving then that they were about to come and take him by force to make him king, Jesus withdrew again to the mountain by himself.

252

Jesus Walks on Water

Matthew 14:22-36 (NIV)

You will need:

Actors   Props
    Narrator   Boat
    Disciple
    Jesus
    Peter

Tips:

- Create an area for Jesus to go off and pray
- Turn a table upside down and cover it with a sheet to create a boat. Use a blue sheet to represent the Sea of Galilee.

Set the scene:

Jesus has just fed the 5000 and dismissed the crowd.

Discussion ideas:

- Jesus goes up on the mountain to be alone and spend time with The Father. We see Jesus do this often. He made time for this in His schedule and we should also. Spending time alone with God in prayer strengthens our relationship with God and equips us to meet the challenges of life. Do you make time in your schedule for quiet time with God? When do you usually do it?
- Peter was walking on water until he took his eyes off of Jesus and focused on the storm around him. This story reminds us to keep our focus on Jesus as we go through our tough situations. Can you think of a time when you needed to keep your focus on Jesus to see you through?

Narrator	Immediately Jesus made the disciples get into the boat and go on ahead of him to the other side, while he dismissed the crowd. After he had dismissed them, he went up on a mountainside by himself to pray. Later that night, he was there alone. And the boat was already a considerable distance from land, buffeted by the waves because the wind was against it. Shortly before dawn Jesus went out to them, walking on the lake. When the disciples saw him walking on the lake they were terrified. The disciples cried out in fear...
Disciple	It's a ghost.
Jesus	Take courage! It is I. Don't be afraid.
Peter	Lord, if it's you. Tell me to come to you on the water.
Jesus	Come.
Narrator	Then Peter got down out of the boat, walked on the water and came toward Jesus. But when he saw the wind, he was afraid and, beginning to sink, cried out...
Peter	Lord, save Me!
Narrator	Immediately Jesus reached out his hand and caught him.
Jesus	You of little faith, why did you doubt?
Narrator	And when they climbed into the boat, the wind died down. Then those who were in the boat worshiped him, saying...
Disciple	Truly you are the Son of God.
Narrator	When they had crossed over, they landed at Gennesaret. And when the men of that place recognized Jesus, they sent word to all the surrounding country. People brought all their sick to him and begged him to let the sick just touch the edge of his cloak, and all who touched it were healed.

Jesus Predicts His Death

Matthew 16:21-28 (NIV)

You will need:

Actors   Props

    Narrator

    Jesus

    Peter

    Disciples (non-speaking)

Tips:

- Creating a setting where Jesus can talk with his disciples.

Set the scene:

Jesus is sitting with his disciples and teaching them.

Discussion ideas:

- Peter was trying to protect Jesus from suffering, but Jesus knew that His suffering was necessary to fulfill God's will. Many times our temptations come from our friends and family that are trying to protect us. Remember that sometimes God will call us to a task that requires sacrifice or discomfort. Always seek God's truth before taking the easy way out. Can you think of a situation where people tried to protect someone when they didn't need protecting? What happened?
- Jesus tells the disciples what it means to follow Him. He tells them that they will have to deny themselves, which means to no longer live only for what makes you happy but to think of others. Can you think of a time when you had to do something for someone else that was uncomfortable or inconvenient for you? What happened?

Narrator	From that time on Jesus began to explain to his disciples that he must go to Jerusalem and suffer many things at the hands of the elders, chief priests and teachers of the law, and that he must be killed and on the third day be raised to life. Peter took him aside and began to rebuke him...
Peter	Never, Lord! This shall never happen to you!
Narrator	Jesus turned and said to Peter...
Jesus	Get behind me, Satan! You are a stumbling block to me; you do not have in mind the concerns of God, but merely human concerns.
Narrator	The Jesus said to his disciples...
Jesus	Whoever wants to be my disciple must deny themselves and take up their cross and follow me. For whoever wants to save their life will lose it, but whoever loses their life for me will find it. What good will it be for someone to gain the whole world, yet forfeit their soul? Or what can anyone give in exchange for their soul? For the Son of Man is going to come in his Father's glory with his angels, and then he will reward each person according to what they have done. Truly I tell you, some who are standing here will not taste death before they see the Son of Man coming in his kingdom.

The Parable of the Good Samaritan

Luke 10: 25-37 (NIV)

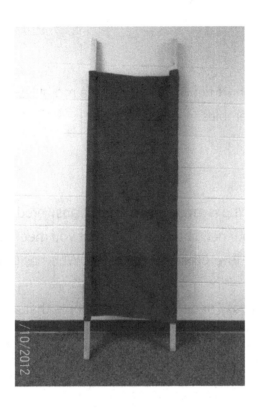

You will need:

Actors

    Narrator

    Expert

    Jesus

    Priest (non-speaking)

    Levite (non-speaking)

    Samaritan (non-speaking)

    Hurt Man (non-speaking)

    Inn Keeper (non-speaking)

Props

    Bandage

    Two Coins

    Stretcher

    Empty jar

Tips from the author:

- Remind the student acting as Jesus to tell the parable slow enough so the other actors can create the drama.
- Use toilet tissue for the bandage if you do not have a medical bandage.
- Use a beach towel for a stretcher if one is not available.

Set the scene:

A parable is a short fictitious story with a moral lesson or principle. Jesus often taught using parables.

Discussion ideas:

- When asked, "Who is my neighbor?" Jesus answered with a parable. The parable teaches that your neighbor is anyone that you meet during your daily activities. God calls us to love others as ourselves. Who has God placed in your life that needs love?
- Do you find it easy or difficult to love people that are different than you? Why or why not?

Narrator	On one occasion an expert in the law stood up to test Jesus.
Expert	Teacher, what must I do to inherit eternal life?
Jesus	What is written in the Law? How do you read it?
Expert	Love the Lord your God with all your heart and with all your soul and with all your strength and with all your mind; and Love your neighbor as yourself.
Jesus	You have answered correctly. Do this and you will live.
Narrator	But he wanted to justify himself, so he asked Jesus...
Expert	And who is my neighbor?
Jesus	A man was going down from Jerusalem to Jericho, when he was attacked by robbers. They stripped him of his clothes, beat him and went away, leaving him half dead. A priest happened to be going down the same road, and when he saw the man, he passed by on the other side. So, too a Levite, when he came to the place and saw him, passed by on the other side. But a Samaritan, as he traveled came where the man was; and when he saw him he took pity on him. He went to him and bandaged his wounds, pouring on oil and wine. Then he put the man on his own donkey, brought him to an inn and took care of him. The next day he took out two denarii and gave them to the innkeeper. Look after him, he said and when I return, I will reimburse you for any extra expense you may have. Which of these three do you think was a neighbor to the man who fell into the hands of robbers?
Expert	The one who had mercy on him.
Jesus	Go and do likewise.

Jesus Raises Lazarus from the Dead

John 11: 1-45 (NIV)

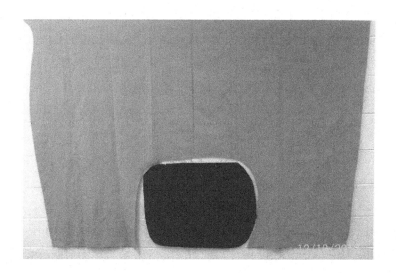

You will need:

Actors

     Narrator

     Jesus

     Disciple

     Thomas

     Martha

     Mary

     Messenger

     Jews (two speaking)

     Lazarus (non-speaking)

Props

     Tomb with a stone

     Cloth or tissue to wrap Lazarus

Tips:

- Designate an area for Mary and Martha's house and an area for the tomb, both in the town of Bethany.
- Designate an area outside of Bethany for Jesus and the disciples.

- Hang a large piece of cloth with a hole cut out of it for a tomb and cut a stone from cardboard to cover the opening. Place cloth strips or a roll of toilet tissue in the tomb and instruct Lazarus to wrap his head, hands and feet before coming out.

Set the scene:

Jesus was preaching in another town when he received the news of Lazarus's sickness.

Discussion ideas:

- Mary and Martha both blamed Jesus for not being there when Lazarus got sick. When trouble or difficult situations come your way, do you complain and blame God or do you see your situation as an opportunity to honor Him?
- Jesus did bring Lazarus back to life, but not as quickly as Mary and Martha wanted. Sometimes we have to be patient and remember that God's timing is not always in line with our timing.
- God has power over death. We are all going to die a physical death, but if we have placed our faith in Jesus Christ, we will not die a spiritual death. In fact, Jesus told Martha that whoever believes in Him will never die. Isn't that great news? Jesus made a way for us to live forever with Him. Have you placed your faith in Jesus?

Narrator	Now a man named Lazarus was sick. He was from Bethany, the village of Mary and her sister Martha. (This Mary, whose brother Lazarus now lay sick, was the same one who poured perfume on the Lord and wiped his feet with her hair.) So the sisters sent word to Jesus...
Messenger	Lord, the one you love is sick.
Narrator	When he heard this, Jesus said...
Jesus	This sickness will not end in death. No, it is for God's glory so that God's Son may be glorified through it.
Narrator	Now Jesus loved Martha and her Sister and Lazarus. So when he heard that Lazarus was sick, he stayed where he was two more days, and then he said to his disciples...
Jesus	Let us go back to Judea.
Disciple	But Rabbi, a short while ago the Jews there tried to stone you and yet you are going back?
Jesus	Are there not 12 hours of daylight? Anyone who walks in the daytime will not stumble, for they see by this world's light. It is when a person walks at night that they stumble, for they have no light. Our friend Lazarus has fallen asleep; but I am going there to wake him up.
Disciple	Lord, if he sleeps, he will get better.
Narrator	Jesus had been speaking of his death, but his disciples thought he meant natural sleep. So then he told them plainly...
Jesus	Lazarus is dead, and for your sake I am glad I was not there, so that you may believe. But let us go to him.
Thomas	Let us also go, that we may die with him.

Narrator	On his arrival, Jesus found that Lazarus had already been in the tomb for four days. Now Bethany was less than two miles from Jerusalem, and many Jews had come to Martha and Mary to comfort them in the loss of their brother. When Martha heard that Jesus was coming, she went out to meet him, but Mary stayed at home.
Martha	Lord! If you had been here, my brother would not have died. But I know that even now God will give you whatever you ask.
Jesus	Your brother will rise again.
Martha	I know he will rise again in the resurrection at the last day.
Jesus	I am the resurrection and the life. The one who believes in me will live, even though they die; and whoever lives by believing in me will never die. Do you believe this?
Martha	Yes, Lord, I believe that you are the Messiah, the Son of God, who is to come into the world.
Narrator	And after she said this, she went back and called her sister, Mary aside.
Martha	The Teacher is here, and is asking for you.
Narrator	When Mary heard this, she got up quickly and went to him. Now Jesus had not yet entered the village, but was still at the place where Martha had met him. When the Jews who had been with Mary in the house, comforting her, noticed how quickly she got up and went out, they followed her, supposing she was going to the tomb to mourn there. When Mary reached the place where Jesus was and saw him, she fell at his feet and said...
Mary	Lord, if you had been here, my brother would not have died.
Narrator	When Jesus saw her weeping, and the Jews who had come along with her also weeping, he was deeply moved in spirit and troubled.
Jesus	Where have you laid him?

Mary	Come and see, Lord.

| Narrator | Jesus wept. |

| Jew 1 | See how he loved him. |

| Jew 2 | Could not he who opened the eyes of the blind man have kept this man from dying? |

| Narrator | Jesus, once more deeply moved, came to the tomb. It was a cave with a stone laid across the entrance. |

| Jesus | Take away the stone. |

| Martha | But, Lord, by this time there is a bad odor, for he has been there four days. |

| Jesus | Did I not tell you that if you believed, you would see the glory of God? |

| Narrator | So they took away the stone. Then Jesus looked up and said... |

| Jesus | Father, I thank you that you have heard me. I knew that you always hear me. But I say this for the benefit of the people standing here, that they may believe that you sent me. |

| Narrator | When he had said this, Jesus called in a loud voice... |

| Jesus | Lazarus, come out! |

| Narrator | The dead man came out, his hands and feet wrapped with strips of linen, and a cloth around his face. |

| Jesus | Take off the grave clothes and let him go. |

| Narrator | Therefore many of the Jews who had come to visit Mary, and had seen what Jesus did, believed in him. |

Jesus Heals the Blind Beggar

Mark 10: 46-52 (NIV)

You will need:

Actors   Props

    Narrator

    Bartimaeus

    Jesus

    Crowd (one speaking)

Tips:

- Create a road with a tan sheet and have Bartimaeus sitting by it.

Set the scene:

Jesus and his disciples were passing through Jericho on their way to Jerusalem.

Discussion ideas:

- How often do we pray for things without really having faith that God will answer our prayers? The blind man had faith as he shouted out to Jesus and Jesus told him it was his faith that healed him.
- How do beggars get treated today? Are they considered a lower class in our socio-economic system? This man was different than most, yet Jesus cared for him. Jesus took the time to call for him, speak to him, and heal him. Do you know anyone who is different? Do they get picked on or treated differently? Jesus cares for them and He wants us to do the same.
- Do you think the people in the crowd were amazed when Jesus made the blind man be able to see? Jesus kept performing miracle after miracle so that people would know He was the messiah and believe. What has God done for you or people you know? We can use those stories, or testimonies, to tell others about Him and help them have faith and believe in Jesus.

Narrator   Then they came to Jericho. As Jesus and his disciples, together with a large crowd, were leaving the city, a blind man, Bartimaeus (which means "Son of Timaeus") was sitting by the roadside begging. When he heard that it was Jesus of Nazareth, he began to shout...

Bartimaeus   Jesus, Son of David, have mercy on me!

Narrator   Many rebuked him and told him to be quiet, but he shouted all the more...

Bartimaeus   Son of David, have mercy on me!

Narrator   Jesus stopped and said...

Jesus   Call him.

Narrator   So they called to the bind man...

Crowd   Cheer up! On your feet! He's calling you.

Narrator   Throwing his cloak aside, he jumped to his feet and came to Jesus.

Jesus   What do you want me to do for you?

Bartimaeus   Rabbi, I want to see.

Jesus   Go, your faith has healed you.

Narrator   Immediately he received his sight and followed Jesus along the road.

Zacchaeus the Tax Collector

Luke 19:1-10 (NIV)

You will need:

Actors	Props
Narrator	Tree
Jesus	
Zacchaeus	
People	

Tips:

- You can put a large plant on top of a table to create a tree for Zacchaeus.

Set the scene:

Zacchaeus was a Jew who chose to become a tax collector for Rome. Tax collectors were known for cheating the Jews, so he was hated by his own people.

Discussion ideas:

- There are people in every society that are hated because of their lifestyle. Zacchaeus was hated by his own people, but he was loved by God. Can you think of anyone or any group of people that live in your area that are hated because of their lifestyle? God has called us to love everyone, even those that are not easy to love.
- Zacchaeus was seeking Jesus. He was short and there was a crowd, but he didn't give up. He found a tree to climb so he could see Jesus. The Bible tells us that if we seek Him, we will find Him. Zacchaeus not only got to see Jesus from a far, he got to spend time with him at his house. Do you ever feel like God is far away? We need to remember to seek Him and not give up. What are some of the ways we can seek Him today?

Narrator	Jesus entered Jericho and was passing through. A man was there by the name of Zacchaeus; he was a chief tax collector and was wealthy. He wanted to see who Jesus was, but because he was short he could not see over the crowd. So he ran ahead and climbed a sycamore-fig tree to see him, since Jesus was coming that way. When Jesus reached the spot, he looked up and said to him...
Jesus	Zacchaeus, come down immediately. I must stay at your house today.
Narrator	So he came down at once and welcomed him gladly. All the people saw this and began to mutter...
People	He has gone to be the guest of a sinner.
Narrator	But Zacchaeus stood up and said to the Lord...
Zacchaeus	Look, Lord! Here and now I give half of my possessions to the poor, and if I have cheated anybody out of anything, I will pay back four times the amount.
Jesus	Today salvation has come to this house, because this man, too, is a son of Abraham. For the Son of Man came to seek and to save the lost.

Jesus Clears the Temple

John 2: 13-22 (NIV)

You will need:

Actors   Props

    Narrator   Coins

    Jesus   Animals to sacrifice

    Disciples   Rope (for a whip)

    Jew

Tips:

- Use stuffed animals or pictures of animals for the sacrifices.
- Use small folding tables (TV trays) for the tables in the temple.

Set the scene:

The Jews were coming to Jerusalem to celebrate the Passover. The Passover is celebrated every year to remember their deliverance from Egypt.

Discussion ideas:

- Jesus was angry that the temple was being used for so many things that people were finding it difficult to worship. Do you think churches today are guilty of this same offense? We need to be sure that when we attend church for worship services that we make worship the main priority.
- Jesus wanted the temple to be used for worship and the people were using it as a market place. In what other ways can you think of that we might displease God at church today? What about talking and socializing when a church leader is teaching? What are some things we can do to keep worship the main priority when we come to church?

Narrator	When it was almost time for the Jewish Passover, Jesus went up to Jerusalem. In the temple courts he found people selling cattle, sheep and doves, and others sitting at tables exchanging money. So he made a whip out of cords and drove all from the temple courts, both sheep and cattle, he scattered the coins of the money changers and overturned their table. To those who sold doves he said…
Jesus	Get these out of here! Stop turning my Father's house into a market!
Narrator	His disciples remembered that it is written.
Disciple	Zeal for your house will consume me.
Narrator	The Jews then responded to him…
Jew	What sign can you show us to prove your authority to do all this.
Jesus	Destroy this temple and I will raise it again in three days.
Jew	It has taken forty-six years to build this temple, and you are going to raise it in three days.
Narrator	But the temple he had spoken of was his body. After he was raised from the dead, his disciples recalled what he had said. Then they believed the Scripture and the words that Jesus had spoken.

Jesus Rides into Jerusalem on a Donkey

Matthew 21: 1-11 (NIV)

You will need:

Actors   Props

  Narrator   Donkey

  Jesus   Coats

  Crowd 1 (one speaker)   Palm Branches

  Crowd 2 (one speaker)

  Reader

  Disciples (non-speaking)

Tips from the author:

- Designate an area for Jerusalem. Have one crowd travel with Jesus from Jericho and the other crowd in Jerusalem.
- Let the reader read from a scroll.
- Use branches from any available tree to represent the palm branches.
- Use a stick horse for the donkey if you have one. Otherwise, use a stuffed animal or just pretend.

Set the scene:

Jesus and the disciples are traveling from Jericho to Jerusalem.

Discussion ideas:

- Jesus was celebrated as he made his triumphal entry. Today we celebrate this event on Palm Sunday. Does your family do anything special to celebrate Palm Sunday or during the following week, to prepare for the Easter Celebration? If so, what?

- Jesus normally didn't make this kind of grand exhibition? Why do you think He did on this occasion? He did it to fulfil a prophecy (read by the reader in the drama). Notice that the crowd was giving the glory to the Lord in the highest heaven. Jesus is a good example to us of always giving the glory to God and not to ourselves.

Narrator   As they approached Jerusalem and came to Bethphage on the Mount of Olives, Jesus sent two disciples, saying to them...

Jesus   Go to the village ahead of you, and at once you will find a donkey tied there, with her colt by her. Untie them and bring them to me. If anyone says anything to you, say that the Lord needs them, and he will send them right away.

Narrator   This took place to fulfill what was spoken through the prophet.

Reader   Say to the Daughter of Zion, See, your king comes to you, gentle and riding on a donkey, on a colt, the foal of a donkey.

Narrator   The disciples went and did as Jesus had instructed them. They brought the donkey and the colt and placed their cloaks on them for Jesus to sit on. A very large crowd spread their cloaks on the road, while others cut branches from the trees and spread them on the road. The crowds that went ahead of him and those that followed shouted...

Crowd 1   Hosanna to the Son of David!
Blessed is he who comes in the name of the Lord!
Hosanna in the highest heaven!

Narrator   When Jesus entered Jerusalem, the whole city was stirred and asked...

Crowd 2   Who is this?

Crowd 1   This is Jesus, the prophet from Nazareth in Galilee

The Last Supper and Betrayal

Matthew 26:1-75 (NKJ)

You will need:

Actors

    Narrator

    Jesus

    Peter

    Judas

    Priest

    2 Girls

    Crowd (one speaks)

    Disciples (one speaks)

    Woman (non-speaking)

    Guards to arrest Jesus

      (non-speaking)

Props

    Juice

    Bread

    Table

    Bag of 30 coins

    Flask / Jar

    Swords & Clubs

Tips:

- Create several settings for this drama: a palace for the Chief Priest, a house in Bethany, house in the city for The Last Supper, the Mount of Olives, Gethsemane, a courtyard. Label each location with a sign so the students will be able to find the locations easily.
- Remind the students that this is a drama and they should act out the scene without hurting each other.

Set the scene:

The time is near for Jesus to die for our sins and He is talking with His disciples.

Discussion ideas:

- Even His disciples disowned Jesus after claiming that they never would. Have you ever been in a situation where you were tempted to disown Jesus? How about remaining silent instead of speaking up for the right thing?
- Jesus was in anguish over the pain He knew was approaching, and He went to be alone with God to pray. Do you make time to be alone with God and pray over situations that worry you? Because of the anguish that Jesus felt, He can relate to our struggles.
- Jesus was willing to obey God even though He knew that what he was about to do would be very painful. His willingness to obey came from his relationship with God. Like Jesus, we should be ready and willing to obey God at all costs.

Narrator	Now it came to pass, when Jesus had finished all these sayings, that He said to His disciples...
Jesus	You know that after two days is the Passover, and the Son of Man will be delivered up to be crucified.
Narrator	Then the chief priests, the scribes, and the elders of the people assembled at the palace of the High priest, who was called Caiaphas, and plotted to take Jesus by trickery and kill him. But they said...
Priest	Not during the feast, lest there be an uproar among the people.
Narrator	And when Jesus was in Bethany at the house of Simon the leper, a woman came to Him having an alabaster flask of very costly fragrant Oil, and she poured it on His head as He sat at the table. But when His disciples saw it, they were indignant, saying...
Disciple	Why this waste? For this fragrant oil might have been sold for much and given to the poor.
Narrator	But when Jesus was aware of it. He said to them...
Jesus	Why do you trouble the woman? For she has done a good work for Me. For you have the poor with you always, but Me you do not have always. For in pouring the fragrant oil on My body, she did it for My burial. Assuredly, I say to you, wherever this gospel is preached in the whole world, what this woman has done will also be told as a memorial to her.
Narrator	Then one of the twelve, called Judas Iscariot, went to the chief priests and said...
Judas	What are you willing to give me if I deliver Him to you?
Narrator	And they counted out to him thirty pieces of silver. So from that time he sought opportunity to betray Him. Now on the first day of the Feast of Unleavened Bread the disciples came to Jesus, saying to Him...

Disciple   Where do You want us to prepare for You to eat the Passover?

Jesus   Go into the city to a certain man, and say to him, 'The Teacher says, "My time is at hand; I will keep the Passover at your house with My disciples.

Narrator   So the disciples did as Jesus had directed them; and they prepared the Passover. When evening had come, He sat down with the twelve. Now as they were eating, He said...

Jesus   Assuredly, I say to you, one of you will betray Me.

Narrator   And they were exceedingly sorrowful, and each of them began to say to Him...

Disciple   Lord, is it I?

Jesus   He who dipped his hand with Me in the dish will betray Me. The Son of Man indeed goes just as it is written of Him, but woe to that man by whom the Son of Man is betrayed! It would have been good for that man if he had not been born.

Narrator   Then Judas, who was betraying Him, answered and said...

Judas   Rabbi, is it I?

Jesus   You have said it.

Narrator   And as they were eating, Jesus took bread, blessed and broke it, and gave it to the disciples and said...

Jesus   Take, eat; this is My body.

Narrator   Then He took the cup, and gave thinks, and gave it to them, saying...

Jesus   Drink from it, all of you. For this is My blood of the new covenant, which is shed for many for the remission of sins. But I say to you, I will not drink of this fruit of the vine from now on until that day when I drink it new with you in My Father's kingdom.

Narrator	And when they had sung a hymn, they went out to the Mount of Olives. Then Jesus said to them...
Jesus	All of you will be made to stumble because of Me this night, for it is written: I will strike the Shepherd, and the sheep of the flock will be scattered. But after I have been raised, I will go before you to Galilee.
Peter	Even if all are made to stumble because of You, I will never be made to stumble.
Jesus	Assuredly, I say to you that this night, before the rooster crows, you will deny Me three times.
Peter	Even if I have to die with You, I will not deny You!
Narrator	And so said all the disciples. Then Jesus came with them to a place called Gethsemane, and said to the disciples...
Jesus	Sit here while I go and pray over there.
Narrator	And He took with Him Peter and the two sons of Zebedee, and He began to be sorrowful and deeply distressed. Then He said to them...
Jesus	My soul is exceedingly sorrowful, even to death. Stay here and watch with Me.
Narrator	He went a little farther and fell on His face, and prayed, saying...
Jesus	O My Father, if it is possible let this cup pass from Me; nevertheless, not as I will, but as You will.
Narrator	Then He came to the disciples and found them sleeping, and said to Peter.
Jesus	What? Could you not watch with Me one hour? Watch and pray, lest you enter into temptation. The spirit indeed is willing, but the flesh is weak.

Narrator   Again, a second time, He went away and prayed, saying...

Jesus   O My Father, if this cup cannot pass away from Me unless I drink it, Your will be done.

Narrator   And he came and found them asleep again, for their eyes were heavy. So He left them, went away again, and prayed the third time, saying the same words. Then He came to His disciples and said to them...

Jesus   Are you still sleeping and resting? Behold, the hour is at hand, and the Son of Man is being betrayed into the hands of sinners. Rise, let us be going. See, My betrayer is at hand.

Narrator   And while He was still speaking, behold, Judas, one of the twelve, with a great multitude with swords and clubs, came from the chief priests and elders of the people. Now His betrayer had given them a sign, saying...

Judas   Whomever I kiss, He is the One; seize Him.

Narrator   Immediately he went up to Jesus and said...

Judas   Greetings, Rabbi!.

Narrator   And kissed Him. But Jesus said to him...

Jesus   Friend, why have you come?

Narrator   Then they came and laid hands on Jesus and took Him. And suddenly, one of those who were with Jesus stretched out his hand and drew his sword, struck the servant of the high priest, and cut off his ear. But Jesus said to him...

Jesus   Put your sword in its place, for all who take the sword will perish by the sword.   Or do you think that I cannot now pray to My Father, and He will provide Me with more than twelve legions of angles? How then could the Scripture be fulfilled, that it must happen thus?

Narrator	In that hour Jesus said to the multitudes...
Jesus	Have you come out, as against a robber, with swords and clubs to take Me? I sat daily with you, teaching in the temple, and you did not seize Me. But all this was done that the Scriptures of the prophets might be fulfilled.
Narrator	Then all the disciples forsook Him and fled. And those who had laid hold of Jesus led Him away to Caiaphas the high priest, where the scribes and the elders were assembled. But Peter followed Him at a distance to the high priest's courtyard. And he went in and sat with the servants to see the end. Now the chief priests, the elders, and all the council sought false testimony against Jesus to put Him to death, but found none. Even though many false witnesses came forward, they found none. But at last two false witnesses came forward and said...
Crowd	This fellow said, I am able to destroy the temple of God and to build it in three days.
Narrator	And the high priest arose and said to Him...
Priest	Do You answer nothing? What is it these men testify against You?
Narrator	But Jesus kept silent. And the high priest answered and said to Him...
Priest	I put You under oath by the living God: Tell us if You are the Christ, the Son of God!
Jesus	It is as you said. Nevertheless, I say to you, hereafter you will see the Son of Man, sitting at the right hand of the Power, and coming on the clouds of heaven.
Narrator	Then the high priest tore his clothes, saying...
Priest	He has spoken blasphemy! What further need do we have of witnesses? Look, now you have heard His blasphemy! What do you think?
Narrator	They answered and said...

Crowd	He is deserving of death.
Narrator	Then they spat in His face and beat Him; and others struck Him with the palms of their hands, saying...
Crowd	Prophesy to us, Christ! Who is the one who struck You?
Narrator	Now Peter sat outside in the courtyard. And a servant girl came to him, saying...
Girl 1	You also were with Jesus of Galilee.
Narrator	But he denied it before them all, saying...
Peter	I do not know what you are saying.
Narrator	And when he had gone out to the gateway, another girl saw him and said to those who were there...
Girl 2	This fellow also was with Jesus of Nazareth.
Narrator	But again he denied with an oath...
Peter	I do not know the Man!
Narrator	And a little later those who stood by came up and said to Peter...
Crowd	Surely you also are one of them, for your speech betrays you.
Narrator	Then he began to curse and swear, saying...
Peter	I do not know the Man!
Narrator	Immediately a rooster crowed. And Peter remembered the word of Jesus who had said to him, 'Before the rooster crows, you will deny Me three times.' So he went out and wept bitterly.

Jesus is Crucified

Matthew 27: 11-66 (NKJ)

You will need:

Actors

       Narrator

       Jesus

       Pilate

       Messenger

       Chief Priest

       Crowd

       Governor

       Centurian

       2 robbers (non-speaking)

       Guard for tomb (non-speaking)

       Joseph (non-speaking)

Props

       Scarlet robe

       Whip or rope for flogging

       Crown of thorns

       Cross

       Sign "This is Jesus, King of the Jews"

       Stones for casting lots

       Clothes

       Curtain (cut in two pieces)

       Pitcher or bottle of water (for Pilate)

Tips:

- Create several settings for this drama: Governor's courtyard (Jesus on trial), Praetorium (Jesus mocked and beaten), Golgotha (Jesus is hung on cross), and Tomb (Jesus is buried).
- Create a temple with a curtain. Cut the curtain in half and put it back together with Velcro so it can be pulled apart. No action takes place there, but the curtain splits when Jesus dies, and this is significant.
- Mark two stones for the soldiers to cast lots for Jesus's clothes. Mark one side of each stone and let them toss them like dice.
- Make a simple cross from a 2x4 board, or even sticks or branches from a tree. Have the students stand in front of it with their arms stretched out.
- As Jesus dies, flash the lights to simulate an earthquake and pull the curtain apart.
- Hang a large piece of cloth with a hole cut out for a tomb and cut a stone from cardboard to cover the opening.
- Even if there are no crosses for the robbers, have two students stand on either side of the cross with their arms also stretched out.

Set the scene:

Jesus has made His triumphal entry into Jerusalem and has had His last supper with His disciples. Judas betrayed Jesus and gave him up to the soldiers, who brought him to the governor and high priest.

Discussion ideas:

- Sometimes people make fun of Christians and their faith. Jesus was mocked and beaten as severe as any one of us and certainly knows what we are feeling in these situations. We need to remember to turn to God for courage when we are feeling mocked for our faith. Have you ever felt like people were mocking you because of your Christian faith?
- At Jesus' death, the massive, thick curtain in the temple in Jerusalem ripped in two. This curtain sealed off the Most Holy Place and no one except the high priest was allowed into the presence of God in that Most Holy Place. The torn

curtain is a reminder that because of Jesus' death on the cross, we all have access to God. What does that mean for us today?

- On the cross, Jesus cried out "Father, why have you forsaken me?" This is what Jesus dreaded as he prayed to God in the garden. Jesus suffered this agonizing death and spiritual separation from God so that we would never have to experience eternal separation from God. What does that mean for us today? Do you believe that Jesus died for you?

Narrator	Now Jesus stood before the governor. And the governor asked Him, saying...
Governor	Are You the King of the Jews?
Jesus	It is as you say.
Narrator	And while He was being accused by the chief priests and elders, He answered nothing. Then Pilate said to Him...
Pilate	Do You not hear how many things they testify against You?
Narrator	But He answered him not one word, so that the governor marveled greatly. Now at the feast the governor was accustomed to releasing to the multitude one prisoner whom they wished. And at that time they had a notorious prisoner called Barabbas. Therefore, when they had gathered together, Pilate said to them...
Pilate	Whom do you want me to release to you? Barabbas, or Jesus who is called Christ?
Narrator	For he knew that they had handed Him over because of envy. While he was sitting on the judgment seat, his wife sent to him, saying...
Messenger	Have nothing to do with that just Man, for I have suffered many things today in a dream because of Him.
Narrator	But the chief priests and elders persuaded the multitudes that they should ask for Barabbas and destroy Jesus. The governor answered and said to them...
Governor	Which of the two do you want me to release to you?
Crowd	Barabbas!
Pilate	What then shall I do with Jesus who is called Christ?
Crowd	Let Him be crucified!

Governor   Why, what evil has He done?

Crowd   Let Him be crucified!

Narrator   When Pilate saw that he could not prevail at all, but rather that a tumult was rising, he took water and washed his hands before the multitude, saying...

Pilate   I am innocent of the blood of this just Person. You see to it.

Narrator   And all the people answered and said...

Crowd   His blood be on us and on our children.

Narrator   Then he released Barabbas to them; and when he had scourged Jesus, he delivered Him to be crucified. Then the soldiers of the governor took Jesus into the Praetorium and gathered the whole garrison around Him. And they stripped Him and put a scarlet robe on Him. When they had twisted a crown of thorns, they put it on His head, and a reed in His right hand. And they bowed the knee before Him and mocked Him, saying...

Crowd   Hail, King of the Jews!

Narrator   Then they spat on Him, and took the reed and struck Him on the head. And when they had mocked Him, they took the robe off Him, put His own clothes on Him, and led Him away to be crucified. Now as they came out, they found a man of Cyrene, Simon by name. Him they compelled to bear His cross. And when they had come to a place called Golgotha, that is to say, Place of a Skull, they gave Him sour wine mingled with gall to drink. But when He had tasted it, He would not drink. Then they crucified Him, and divided His garments, casting lots, that it might be fulfilled which was spoken by the prophet: "They divided My garments among them, and for My clothing they cast lots." Sitting down, they kept watch over Him there. And they put up over His head the accusation written against Him: THIS IS JESUS THE KING OF THE JEWS. Then two robbers were crucified with Him, one on the right and another on the left. And those who passed by blasphemed Him, wagging their heads and saying...

Crowd   You who destroy the temple and build it in three days, save Yourself! If You are the Son of God, come down from the cross.

Narrator   Likewise the chief priests also, mocking with the scribes and elders said...

Chief Priest He saved others; Himself He cannot save. If He is the king of Israel, let Him now come down from the cross, and we will believe Him. He trusted in God; let Him deliver Him now if He will have Him; for He said, 'I am the Son of God.'

Narrator   Even the robbers who were crucified with Him reviled Him with the same thing. Now from the sixth hour until the ninth hour there was darkness over all the land. And about the ninth hour Jesus cried out with a loud voice, saying...

Jesus   Eli, Eli, lama sabachthani? My God, My God, why have You forsaken Me?

Narrator   Some of those who stood there, when they heard that, said...

Crowd   This Man is calling For Elijah!

Narrator   Immediately one of them ran and took a sponge, filled it with sour wine and put it on a reed, and offered it to Him to drink.

Crowd   Let Him alone; let us see if Elijah will come to save Him.

Narrator   And Jesus cried out again with a loud voice, and yielded up His spirit. Then, behold, the veil of the temple was torn in two from top to bottom; and the earth quaked, and the rocks were split. And the graves were opened; and many bodies of the saints who had fallen asleep were raised; and coming out of the graves after His resurrection, they went into the holy city and appeared to many. So when the centurion and those with him, who were guarding Jesus, saw the earthquake and the things that had happened, they feared greatly, saying...

Centurian   Truly this was the Son of God!

Narrator   And many women who followed Jesus from Galilee, ministering to Him, were there looking on from afar, among who were Mary Magdalene, Mary the mother of James and Joses, and the mother of Zebedee's sons. Now when evening had come, there came a rich man from Arimathea, named Joseph, who himself had also become a disciple of Jesus. This man went to Pilate and asked for the body of Jesus. Then Pilate commanded the body to be given to him. When Joseph had taken the body, he wrapped it in a clean linen cloth, and laid it in his new tomb which he had hewn out of the rock; and he rolled a large stone against the door of the tomb, and departed. And Mary Magdalene was there, and the other Mary, sitting opposite the tomb. On the next day, which followed the Day of Preparation, the chief priests and Pharisees gathered together to Pilate, saying...

Chief Priest   Sir, we remember, while He was still alive, how that deceiver said. "After three days I will rise." Therefore command that the tomb be made secure until the third day, lest His disciples come by night and steal Him away, and say to the people, 'He has risen from the dead.' So the last deception will be worse than the first.

Pilate   You have a guard; go your way, make it as secure as you know how.

Narrator   So they went and made the tomb secure, sealing the stone and setting the guard.

The Resurrection

Matthew 28: 1-20, Luke 24:50-53 (NKJ)

11/10/2012

You will need:

Actors

    Narrator

    Angel

    Jesus

    Elders

    Chief Priest (non-speaking)

    Mary Magdalene (non-speaking)

    Mary Mother of Jesus
       (non-speaking)

    Two Guards (non-speaking)

    Disciples (non-speaking)

Props

    Jars (of spices)

    tomb

    bag of money

Tips:

- Hang a large piece of cloth with a hole cut out of it for a tomb and cut a stone from cardboard to cover the opening.

Set the scene:

> Jesus has been crucified and buried in the tomb. The chief priest had guards posted at the tomb so no one could come and take the body because Jesus had told them that he would rise after three days.

Discussion ideas:

- Jesus' resurrection is very significant to the Christian faith. It shows us that we have a living savior. Jesus was not a false prophet or an imposter. Just as He promised, He died for our sins and rose again. Death is not the end. We, too, can live eternally because of Jesus, by believing in His finished work on the cross. We believe in Jesus and He gives us Eternal Life. Do you believe in Jesus?
- Jesus gave the disciples the Great Commission: to go and make disciples of all nations, baptizing them in the name of the Father and of the Son and of the Holy Spirit and teaching them to obey everything I have commanded you. How can we follow this command today?

Narrator   Now after the Sabbath, as the first day of the week began to dawn, Mary Magdalene and the other Mary came to see the tomb. And behold, there was a great earthquake; for an angel of the Lord descended from heaven, and came and rolled back the stone from the door, and sat on it. His countenance was like lightning, and his clothing as white as now. And the guards shook for fear of him, and became like dead men. But the angel answered and said to the women...

Angel   Do not be afraid, for I know that you seek Jesus who was crucified. He is not here; for He is risen, as He said. Come, see the place where the Lord lay. And go quickly and tell His disciples that He is risen from the dead, and indeed He is going before you into Galilee; there you will see Him, Behold, I have told you.

Narrator   So they went out quickly from the tomb with fear and great joy, and ran to bring His disciples word. And as they went to tell His disciples, behold, Jesus met them, saying...

Jesus   Rejoice!

Narrator   So they came and held Him by the feet and worshiped Him. Then Jesus said to them...

Jesus   Do not be afraid. Go and tell My brethren to go to Galilee, and there they will see Me.

Narrator   Now while they were going, behold, some of the guards came into the city and reported to the chief priests all the things that had happened. When they had assembled with the elders and consulted together, they gave a large sum of money to the soldiers, saying...

Elders   Tell them, His disciples came at night and stole Him away while we slept. And if this comes to the governor's ears, we will appease him and make you secure.

Narrator   So they took the money and did as they were instructed; and this saying is commonly reported among the Jews until this day. Then the eleven disciples went away into Galilee, to the mountain which Jesus had appointed for them.

When they saw Him, they worshiped Him; but some doubted. And Jesus came and spoke to them, saying...

Jesus   All authority has been given to Me in heaven and on earth. Go therefore and make disciples of all the nations, baptizing them in the name of the Father and of the Son and of the Holy Spirit, teaching them to observe all things that I have commanded you, and lo, I am with you always, even to the end of the age.

Narrator   And He led them out as far as Bethany, and He lifted up His hands and blessed them. Now it came to pass, while He blessed them, that He was parted from them and carried up into heaven. And they worshiped Him, and returned to Jerusalem with great joy, and were continually in the temple praising and blessing God. Amen.

The Holy Spirit Comes at Pentecost

Acts 2: 1-21, 37-47 (NIV)

You will need:

Actors   Props

    Narrator   Fan

    Crowd (one speaking)   Fire

    Peter

Tips:

- Use a fan for the wind.
- Cut flames from red and orange paper.

Set the scene:

Jesus has been crucified and buried and he rose from the tomb. He appeared to his disciples before ascending to heaven. He gave them the Great Commission and told them to stay in the city until they could be clothed with power form on high.

Discussion ideas:

- At Pentecost, fire came down on many believers, symbolizing that God's presence is now available to all who believe in him. As Peter addressed the crowd, he explained that everyone who believes will receive the gift of the Holy Spirit. What does this mean for us today?
- In what ways can you tell that the Holy Spirit still dwells within people today?
- Those last few verses give us a picture of what the church should look like. Do you see any similarities to churches today? The believers came together for fellowship, shared meals, praised God and ministered to each other. Does that sound like churches today?

Narrator	When the day of Pentecost came, they were all together in one place. Suddenly a sound like the blowing of a violent wind came from heaven and filled the whole house where they were sitting. They saw what seemed to be tongues of fire that separated and came to rest on each of them. All of them were filled with the Holy Spirit and began to speak in other tongues as the Spirit enabled them. Now they were staying in Jerusalem God-fearing Jews from every nation under heaven. When they heard this sound, a crowd came together in bewilderment, because each one heard their own language being spoken. Utterly amazed, they asked...
Crowd	Aren't all these who are speaking Galileans? Then how is it that each of us hears them in his own native language? Parthians, Medes and Elamites; residents of Mesopotamia, Judea and Cappadocia, Pontus and Asia, Phrygia and Pamphylia, Egypt and the parts of Libya near Cyrene; visitors from Rome, (both Jews and converts to Judaism), Cretans and Arabs—we hear them declaring the wonders of God in our own tongues!
Narrator	Amazed and perplexed, they asked one another...
Crowd	What does this mean?
Narrator	Some, however, made fun of them and said...
Crowd	They have had too much wine.
Narrator	Then Peter stood up with the Eleven, raised his voice and addressed the crowd...
Peter	Fellow Jews and all of you who live in Jerusalem, let me explain this to you; listen carefully to what I say. These people are not drunk, as you suppose. It's only nine in the morning! No, this is what was spoken by the prophet Joel: In the last days, God says, I will pour out my Spirit on all people. Your sons and daughters will prophesy, your young men will see visions, your old men will dream dreams. Even on my servants, both men and women, I will pour out my Spirit in those days, and they will prophesy. I will show wonders in the heaven above and signs on the earth below, blood and fire and billows of smoke. The sun will be turned to darkness and the moon to blood before the coming of

the great and glorious day of the Lord. And anyone who calls on the name of the Lord will be saved.

Narrator   When the people heard this, they were cut to the heart and said to Peter and the other apostles...

Crowd   Brothers, what shall we do?

Peter   Repent and be baptized, every one of you, in the name of Jesus Christ for the forgiveness of your sins. And you will receive the gift of the Holy Spirit. The promise is for you and your children and for all who are far off-for all whom the Lord our God will call.

Narrator   With many other words he warned them; and he pleaded with them.

Peter   Save yourselves from this corrupt generation.

Narrator   Those who accepted his message were baptized, and about three thousand were added to their number that day. They devoted themselves to the apostles' teaching and to fellowship, to the breaking of bread and to prayer. Everyone was filled with awe, and many wonders and signs were done by the apostles. All the believers were together and had everything in common. They sold property and possessions to give to anyone who had need. Every day they continued to meet together in the temple courts. They broke bread in their homes and ate together with glad and sincere hearts, praising God and enjoying the favor of all people. And the Lord added to their number daily those who were being saved.